INSTANT MONEY EMPOWERMENT

by MARIA SOLOMON

2002
ORIGINAL PUBLICATIONS
1 (888) OCCULT - 1

INSTANT MONEY EMPOWERMENT

By Mária Solomon

ISBN: 0-942272-75-7

Please be advised that we cannot make any claims of supernatural effects or powers for any of the formulas, spells, rituals, etc. listed herein. The Author offers the contents for interest, folklore value, experimentation and whatever value it may have to the reader thereof. This book is offered as a Literary Curio Only. No responsibility whatsoever for the contents or the validity of the statements herein is assumed by the author, publisher or seller of this book.

FIRST EDITION
First Printing 2002

Interior illustrations by Mark Taylor

Original Publications
P.O. Box 236
Old Bethpage, New York 11804-0236
(516) 454-6809

Printed in the United States of America

DEDICATION

To my Husband, Howard,
whose love, courageous persistence and perseverance
leads us to greater heights of achievement upon our path.

To my Children:

Rob D'Andrea, whose heart and musical abilities vibrate with the notes of the Universe.

Rick Holecek, whose connection to nature gives his soul wings to fly the Spiritual planes.

Gina Holecek, Rick's wife and my new daughter, who brings love, her bubbling spirit and openness to new experiences and adventures to us all.

To my Mother, Maria Berde, for her persistance towards excellence, creativity and herbal knowledge.

To my Father, Lichtig Laszló, for all his spiritual guidance, love and understanding.

As they walk along their path,
may they continue to receive their blessings with love...

The time is right to elevate yourself and others on the Path of Light. Utilized by us in the higher, inner circles of magi, the information is meant to be used as suggestions in this book. Use the formulae contained in these pages with love, discretion, truth and for only positive purposes. Trust your inner self and use wisdom.

MARÍA SOLOMON

TABLE OF COTENTS

INTRODUCTION

This book is a Light Worker's guide to utilizing ancient tools for modern times. As well as my own proven secret formulae. The forces of nature are there to be worked with in a positive way. Information has been passed down by word of mouth from the ancient wise known by titles such as magis, shamans, priestesses, elders, vitkis and sages. Throughout every age and culture, there have been genuine practitioners of our higher inner circles who continue to work only on the positive Path of Divine Light.

God supplies our every need. If we haven't received prosperity (health, love, money, etc.), it is because our minds haven't connected correctly to the Divine Source yet. Know the Self first and your true connection to the Oneness with God. Your source is always within yourself, not from outward.

Keep your mind on changing negative to positive; love, truth, integrity, harmony, wisdom and abundance. Keep to your Higher Self, to Higher visions. As these changes occur, the Law of Abundance will start to manifest and bring to you what your needs and desires are.

Your mind has to be on love, truth and peace to be unlimited. You are One with God and the indwelling Divine Power is what you need to be aware of. Your job is to be aware, the rest (how, when, where, what will come in) is not in your hands. Trust that all will come.

Once you understand that Divinity manifests through you, you will be unrestricted in your prosperity. Material gain, wealth, health, love, prosperity are the outward forms of inner thoughts. Prosperity is our Divine birth right. It belongs to us. The Source of our supply is unlimited; therefore, we are unlimited.

Remember that money is a way to receive what you need (house, car, etc.). The reality is that once your mind realizes what you need, that need will be supplied. One source of this supply is money. The true supply is your *awareness* of Divine Power and that Divine Power is what your Supply of Abundance actually is. The supply is never ending. Become aware that the creative energies within you are capable and create abundance as the Law dictates. The spirit within is your source. You are connected to God as your only source. Do not look outward - you will find nothing.

The more you give, the more will come to you. Do not be afraid of letting go of material things. They come back ten fold. Give your love and live by the Truth. Live the Law of Abundance and be happy. I have been a psychic and metaphysician on this Path for numerous years. I find the ancient methods are more direct, powerful and simplified. My book contains a mixture of ancient techniques as well as my own special formulae which took years to develop.

As an occultist and psychic, I am aware that anything we can imagine we can manifest. There is a misconception that money is the root of all evil. You need only to look at the Bible or any other form of religious book to see this is not so. As an example, in the Bible it says that the love of money is negative, not money itself. It is only negative when put it first instead of Divine Power. The Bible also states in Genesis 13:2, "Abram was a very right man." It was a positive situation. God never wanted Abram to get rid of his wealth. God wants you to be happy.

You need only to remember that there is a balancing force at work through Divine Power. The balance between the spiritual and material. After all, it would be very difficult to be spiritual and help others if you are starving and need to put all of your energy into survival.

Work only in a positive way. When you gain material success through spiritual work, give something back to the earth and others to keep the prosperity flow and not cancel out what you gained. Do not forget to thank Divine Power through which all things manifest.

You will discover as you develop on your Spiritual Path that you have a strong sense of humor. When you can work with nature to manifest your needs, you will not take situations in your life as seriously.

Work with Divine Power to achieve success.

You can do it!

Get out of the darkness and into the Light.

Step through the door
to gain victory over financial obstacles.

CHAPTER 1

SUCCESSFUL SPELLCRAFTING

All forms of occult culture have the same basis in magick, whether pre-Christian or not, Egyptian mysteries, Kabbalah, Wiccan or any number of ancient traditions. The main purpose in all of these systems is self-awareness and development. The development of the self on all levels, spiritual, mental, emotional and physical. We are more focused on the physical in this book. However, you do need to unify all the levels. In all things, you need harmony and balance. Any valid literature on magick will tell you this. As you peruse any study of the mysteries, look for the balance and self-heightening levels, and work only with the positive side.

When you work magick, you are making changes. Work only for the better. Making these changes must include within yourself. All of our realities come down to a matter of perception. Everything is relevant. If you look at a cool, blue, rippling stream and it makes you feel happy and warm, it may be difficult to understand if some other person cannot wait to get as far as possible from it. Yet, the water and the situation may be exactly the same. The only difference is the perspective of each individual.

The ability to understand how magick functions, transform situations by implementing this higher knowledge and thus achieving goals is what magick is all about. One of the methods used for this purpose is spellcrafting. A spell is an invocation by one of power such as by a magi, ju-ju man, wizard or priestess. This invocation will influence another person or object. Good spells would heighten health, gain knowledge or any positive purpose you can think of. Amulets or varied objects can have spells cast on them. A spell is also a formula or ritual. To gain wealth, you need to combine magick, work and spiritual awareness. Spellcrafting is the ability to do this.

Now get started and set a goal to work towards. Nobody stands in your way now. You are the only one that can cancel your goals. You are also the only one who can achieve them. Nothing can hold you back. You are creating your own reality right now.

You are always under your own control.

MONEY CIRCLE

1. Make a circle out of dollar bills, quarters, dimes, nickels, pennies. It can even be a picture of money from a magazine or from a board game.

2. Stand in the middle of the circle and repeat the following three times:

I weave the spell of success,
Through the strengthening power of prayer,
Financial wealth and excess,
Comes to me direct and will not err.

3. Visualize the circle of money growing and becoming real.

KEY TO SUCCESS

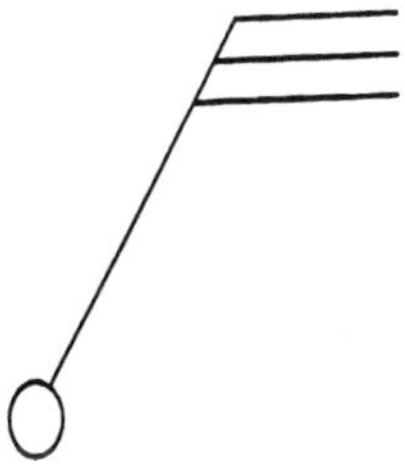

This Umbanda spell is a powerful formula. The Key is the sign of open doors, it let's good things come out and come to you. Draw the symbol depicted in the center of a green cloth using white chalk. As you draw the Key visualize all doors opening to you.

When you've completed the drawing, place a cup of water and a white candle a corner of the cloth. Light the candle and recite the following incantation.

God of earth, God of change,
Bring to me all the treasures of this domain.
I seek to balance and harmonize my life,
To fulfill all of my needs.
With this key I proclaim:
"No obstacles will block, hold nor hinder me."

MONEY BAGS OF WEALTH

1. Take four mojo bags the color of grass green. In each bag place:

   A one dollar bill
   2 quarters
   2 dimes
   2 nickels
   10 pennies

2. Place in the four mojo bags with the money:

   1 Orris root
   1 Buckeye
   1 Pecan nut

3. Tie each bag with white thread three times. While you tie the bag, focus on it and say:

   Money to money,
   Power to power,
   Let the wealth that is mine,
   Through Divine Right be showered,
   Upon my home,
   Upon my work,
   Through rain and thunder,
   From air to earth.

4. Take the bags and place each one into one of the four corners of your home. They can be placed somewhere that is not visual but in the open air, such as under a couch or in a potted plant.

5. Leave them there and visualize your home filled with money.

MAGICKAL DOLL FOR FINANCIAL GAIN

When making a doll, it does not matter what kind you use. One type is not better than another. Make one out of *any* material you have available *(i.e. paper, cloth)*. The doll does not have to be a particular color, however, colors do have attributable vibrations. For the purpose of a financial ritual it is appropriate to use either green, white or orange. When you work with a doll, only use one intent. Do not change it.

1. Cut two pieces of cloth in the outline of a body.

2. Sew the two pieces together leaving a space to fill the doll with the following herbs and stones:

Fenugreek	*2 Turquoise stones*
Chamomile	*1 Pyrite stone*
High John	

3. On a piece of paper write your name seven times in lower case letters and the words:

   Money, money, come to me,
   Through fenugreek and doll of need,
   Bring in silver, bring in gold,
   Bring it fast, to my hand to hold.

4. Place the paper into the doll with the herbs and stones, then stich closed.

5. With white thread, make large stitches to represent the eyes, nose, mouth and heart. Give the doll a name *(it could be yours!)*

6. Repeat the spell verbally for either nine days or until the goal is completed. Dolls have been in use for ages, which tells you that they work.

RUNIC MONEY SPELL

1. Write your need on parchment and place beneath a Green pull-out candle.

2. On another piece of parchmant paper write the following in black ink:

I now affirm that money comes to me
easily and freely all the time.
Divine Sustenance provides for all of my needs. Amen.

3. In the corners draw these Runic symbols in red: (ᚠ, ᚹ, ᛋ) along with these astrological symbols: (♃, ♀)

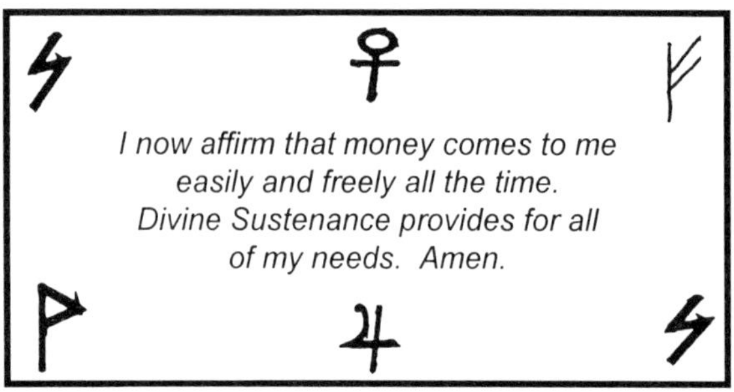

4. Place parchment under incense burner and light an incense blend of Frankincense, Myrrh, Benzoin and Sandalwood on charcoal. Use one teaspoon each and mix them together. Burn 1 teaspoon of the mixture in the incense burner. Leave the parchment under the burner for three hours. When this is done, place the parchment under the green candle.

5. Add more incense into the burner and light your green candle. Allow the candle to burn for seven days and repat this ritual until the goal is attained.

GRAVEYARD DIRT

Legends are numerous about its power for positive and negative work. We are only interested in positive. It is also known as Conjure Dust, Graveyard Dust and Goofer Dust. Graveyard Dirt is sometimes taken from a graveyard but often times it is formulated from a combination of mullein, sumbul or any musky powder of roots or herbs.

WARDING OFF SPELL

Do this spell to cancel negative people who are in your life and blocking you. However, you will do so in a positive way. After all, if you deal with negative people, it will slow down your upward climb to success.

1. Use Graveyard Dirt (or powdered Mullein leaves) and mix with the dirt a small item belonging to the person you want to cancel, such as a comb, some hair, part of a shirt.

2. Wrap the object and dirt in the parchment with white string. Focus on love and sending the person away.

3. Bury it away from your home and say:

Stay from my door,
And don't come near,
Through spirit and earth,
Stay far from here.
Amen.

4. Focus on the person going away and being happy somewhere else. Bless the person and let it go.

PROSPERITY SPELL

One of the herbs used mixed with or as a substitute for Graveyard Dust is named Patchouli. Patchouli smells like the rich earth. It is also connected to the earth element.

To attract prosperity, sprinkle Patchouly onto money that you carry or in your wallet or purse.

Patchouly can also be placed around the base of a green candle.This too, will attract prosperity.

TO OBTAIN MONEY FAST

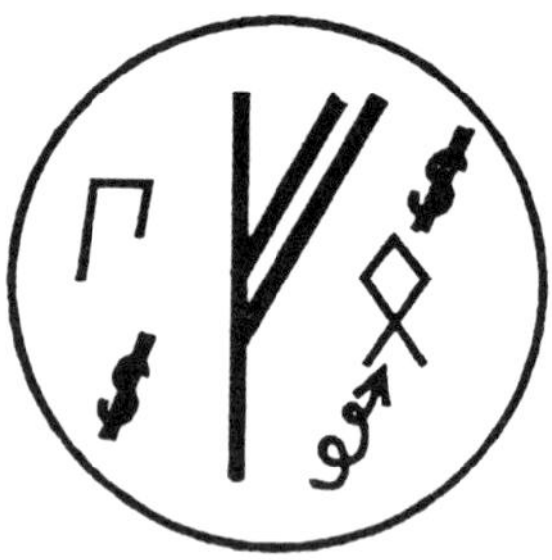

1. Copy this figure onto parchment paper.
2. Focus on your needs and a fast increase in your finances. Anoint the parchment with Fast Luck Oil.
3. Wrap a dollar bill around it and carry it in your wallet

LUCKY MONEY LAVENDER SPELL

1. Sprinkle seven types of money with Lavender and place into a green conjure bag (one penny, one nickel, one dime, one quarter, one half dollar, one dollar bill, one five dollar bill).
2. Anoint your bag with Lavender oil each day and take everywhere you go. It is said that your money should increase soon.

MOJO BAGS

Mojo bags are an important part in Voodoo, shamanic and various forms of magick. There are numerous names for these magical bags, but the intent is always the same. Some names these magical bags are called are: *Mojo bags, Conjure bags, Ouanga, Wishing, Hex, Gris-Gris, Wanga, Medicine bags or Charm bags.* You can buy one already fixed or make your own. If you make your own, choose the correct color for your intent. The most common materials used are leather, cotton, flannel or chamois. Use white thread to sew your bag. While you sew, focus on your purpose the whole time. You can place any number of items into the bag. The items all have to be for the same purpose, such as all for health or money, business, etc. If you purchase a bag, make sure you add something that is personal, such as a strand of hair. Also add your focus/intent. After the mojo bag is finished, anoint it with a corresponding oil.

VOODOO CHARM

Start this ritual on a Thursday, this being the day connected to the voodoo deity Damballah.

1. Focus deeply on your intent. Write your needs on parchment and place it into a green conjure bag along with a High John The Conqueror root and a Talisman of Damballah.

2. Anoint the bag with Money Drawing oil each day at a quiet time when you can focus without interruption. Keep your bag with you.

GOOD LUCK WHEN GAMBLING

Carry 4 Tonka Beans, a pair of Green Lodestones and Gold Magnetic sand in a green flannel bag.

INFLUENCE IN GAMBLING

In a green mojo bag place the following:

1 green rabbit's foot
2 lodestones
Seal of Fortune
Ankh
Lucky Hand
Devil's Shoestring

Tie the mojo bag and anoint it with Fast Luck Oil. Then when you are ready to gamble, use a little of the Fast Luck Oil on the palms of your hands and wrists. Remember to focus your intent.

MONEY DRAWING MOJO BAG

In a red mojo bag place the following: *1 Low John Root, 1 gold lodestone, a small horseshoe, Gold magnetic sand.* Anoint the bag each day with Money Drawing oil and carry with it you.

ANOTHER MONEY DRAWING MOJO BAG

Place some Squill root, one silver dime, one silver quarter and one silver dollar in a flannel bag. Sprinkle the bag with Money Drawing Powder and anoint with Bayberry oil. While burning Money Drawing Incense and a Green candle say the following money drawing prayer:

> *"Father and All Saints, I call on you to help me succeed, as I need the money to help me in my life, please I beg of you, help me draw money, bring me silver, bring me dollars hot or cold."*

(Anoint the bag, burn the candle and the incense each day until you get the assistance you need.)

CHAPTER 2

HOW TO CREATE WHAT YOU NEED WITH NATURAL FORCES

FINANCE DRAWING FROM EARTH AND AIR

1. Write on parchment paper with Dove's Blood Ink (or red ink) what your needs are.

2. Draw the sign of Jupiter within a circle in the dirt or sand. You can use a stick. Focus on expansion.

3. On top of the sign of Jupiter, place the parchment paper.

4. Light it and focus on your intent. Make sure all the paper is burned. You may have to relight it. Let the ashes scatter to the winds. Then rub out the drawing.

FLYING DRAGON SPELL

During a quiet uninterupted time, twice a week on Thursday and Sunday, visualize a giant dragon of green standing guard over hills of gold and silver. Say three times:

Dragon, dragon,
Made of green,
Bring fast money,
Unto me.
Use your speed,
And use your power,
Bring my wealth,
To me this hour.

Next, visualize the dragon guarding YOUR hills of gold and silver for you, as the hills get larger and larger.

SPELL OF THE EARTH ENERGIES

This is a direct tool to bring money and opportunity.

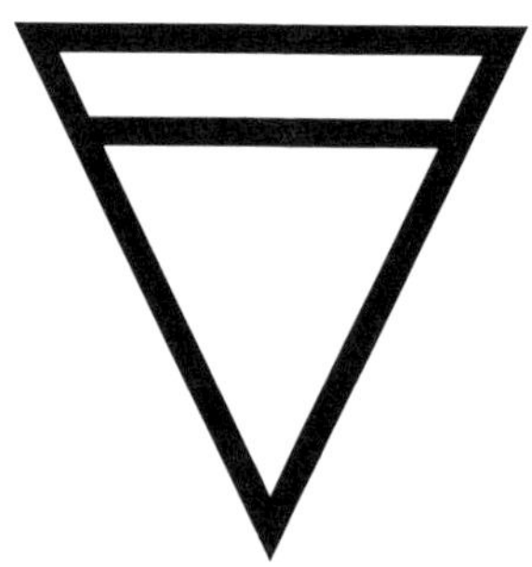

1. Draw this alchemical sign for earth on four pieces of white paper.

2. In your bedroom, place one directly above your head on the wall. The other three on each of the other walls at about the same height.

3. Lay on your bed and focus on drawing a spiral of energy from the symbol above you down through your crown chakra (top of your head), down through your body and out through your feet to each of the other symbols and spiral it back into your solar plexus.

MONEY PROSPERITY RITUAL

1. During a new moon, take a Spiritual Bath. Use a High John the Conqueror Bath. Soak for 20 minutes. While bathing, mentally focus on your money desire.

2. Upon finishing, anoint two green candles with Money Drawing Oil and light them. Next, light Sandalwood Incense.

3. As the smoke floats higher, send your desire out with it. Focus as long as you can then leave the room. Let the candles and incense burn themselves out.

MONEY DRAWING RITUAL

1. At the time of the full moon, go outdoors. It is best to wear something white, also something green.

2. Stand with your arms raised above your head, fingers pointing towards the sky. Stand with your legs apart, comfortably.

3. Visualize the energy from above flowing down through your crown chakra (top of your head), down through your fingers and out towards the Universe. At the same time, do the same from beneath the earth, up through your legs and up through your arms, to your finger tips and out.

4. Now as you send the energy out, visualize your desired request going with it.

5. When you are done with your intent, lower your arms. Thank Divine Power and know that it is done.

FLAME RITUAL FOR MATERIAL GAIN

1. Find a quiet place where you will not be disturbed during your work. Try to do the ritual in the same place each time.

2. Place a table or flat surface where you will be able to make an altar and do the work. On the altar place the following items:

   Cover your surface with a white cloth.

   Something to symbolize your belief system (such as a cross).

   1 white candle, 1 green candle, 1 yellow candle (Place the candles however you prefer, each time you do the Flame Ritual, place the candles in the same spot.)

   An urn or bowl you can light paper in

   Matches

   Incense (any form to attract prosperity)

3. Take a few deep breaths to relax physically and mentally.

   On a piece of white paper, write:

   Through Divine Power (or fill in your word), I now request the following to manifest in a positive way. My request is ____________________________ .
   (Such as a new business, money, a car, etc.)

4. Next, approach the altar. Light the candles and the incense.

(continued)

5. You can fold the paper if you need to and place it with your request in the bowl. Light it and say:

   I now invoke the Power of the Flame, through Divine Power (or your word), to fulfill my desires. I know that as I ask, it is done.

   I invoke the elements of air, earth, water and fire to bring forth into material manifestation all of my requests, NOW!

   In the fire as it rages, my request now goes to the Source. I know the eternal flame now purifies and manifests my needs.

   So Be It!

   Thank you Divine Power (or your own word).

6. The paper needs to be completely burned to ashes if it needs to be reignited, do so.

7. When you are done, put the candles out. Do not blow them out with your breath. Always put them out in the same color order.

8. Take the bowl outside and throw the ashes to the wind. If you throw it away inside, you will cancel the ritual.

TREE RITUAL OF WEALTH

1. Find an oak or maple tree. Sit under the tree with your back touching it. Mentally or verbally repeat seven times:

The elements and I are One, I ask you (the tree),
my brother, to help me to achieve
Power in the physical kingdom.
I need to manifest ____________________ (fill in your need).
Thank you through Divine Power.

2. Get up and circle the tree seven times going clockwise. Focus on your intent.

3. Stop at the place you started. Face the tree. Placing your right palm against the bark, say what your intent is, thank the tree and walk away knowing it is done.

LINK TO THE PAST

1. Perform this ritual before noon. Wear some black and also the color white. On an outdoor fire (can be a camp fire), place a kettle filled with the following:

16 cups water	*2 maple leaves*
8 tbsp. chamomile flowers	*2 turquoise stones*
2 tigers eye stones	*1/2 cup white wine*

2. Bring to a boil. As it steams, look into the steam and make your request.

3. Request it through Divine Power, through earth and air, water and fire.

4. When you are finished, let the water cool. Remove the gemstones and keep them with you at all times. Empty the kettle at the base of a tree.

FULL MOON RITUAL

1. On the night of a full moon, take a Hyssop Spiritual Bath for 20 minutes minimum.

2. Anoint 3 candles with Indian Oil. Line them up next to each other, from left to right in this order: *green, white, orange.* Light all three.

3. Burn Money Drawing Incense while focusing on your intent.

QUICK MONEY FORMULA RITUAL

1. In the sand or dirt at the time of the new moon, draw a triangle.

2. At the left bottom corner, place a glass of water. On the right corner, place the lit incense called Rue. At the top, place $1.90 in change.

3. Focus on your money building. *"See"* it grow. Ask for your intent to work through water, air, earth and sea.

RITUAL OF POWER

1. On an altar, place a white cloth.

2. On top of the cloth place a square-shaped blue cloth.

3. On the blue cloth, place a smaller square of yellow.

4. Place a symbol of your belief *(such as a cross)* on your yellow cloth in the center.

5. Light some Tobacco Incense in the room.

6. Dim the lights and put soft music on (non-verbal).

7. Face north. Stand with your legs apart and your arms raised towards the sky.

8. Invoke the angel Uriel.

9. Make your intent known. Be specific as to what your exact needs are. For what purpose *(such as paying a bill, starting a new job in a specific field or to improve your life)?*

10. When you are done, than the Father and then thank Uriel. Allow the incense to burn itself out.

DIVINE FORCE

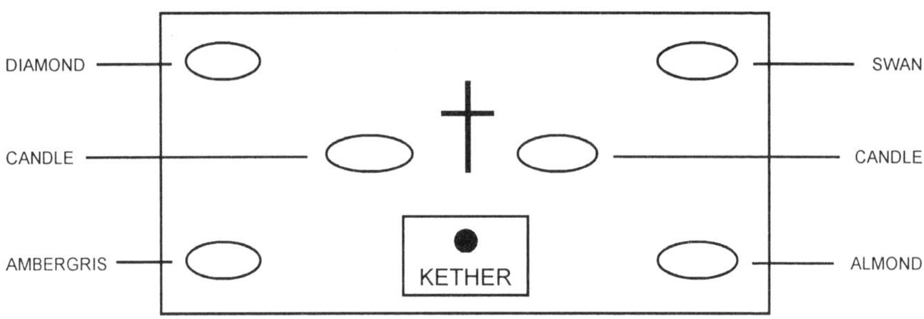

1. Make an altar by covering the surface with a white or purple cloth.

2. On the cloth in the center, place your religious symbol.

3. Place two white candles on the altar. One on each side of the religious symbol.

(continued)

4. Place a replica of a swan in the right upper corner.

5. A diamond in the left upper corner.

6. On the right bottom corner, place an almond. It can be the flower or nut or part of the tree.

7. In the left bottom corner, place the perfume, oil or incense with the smell of Ambergris.

8. On a white paper, place with black ink, a point (dot) in the center. Under this, write the word KETHER. Place the paper in front of your religious symbol.

9. Light the candles and incense (or open the oil to have the aroma in the air). Dim the lights.

10. Recite the following invocation

    I now invoke the power of Metatron,
    Through the force of Eheieh,
    To attain that which rightfully belongs to me,
    Through Divine Right and the Law,
    My desires are (fill in your desire).
    Thank you Eheieh,
    Thank you Metatron.
    So Be It!

11. Put the candles out. Know that it is done.

12. Repeat the ritual as frequently as you want.

13. Carry a piece of paper with the names Metatron and Eheieh and your desires in your wallet or purse at all times.

CHAPTER 3

MAGICKAL TALISMANS

Likened to a sword and a shield, a talisman may be defined as an object which has been magically endowed with the power of attracting good fortune. The word talisman is defined in the *Oxford English Dictionary* as an object engraven with figures or characters to which are attributed the occult powers of the planetary influences and celestial configurations under which it was made; usually worn as an amulet to avert evil or bring fortune to the wearer'. The word is traced to the Greek *telesma,* meaning in this case a consecrated object, one over which a rite has been completed.

HOW TO MAKE A TALISMAN

In making a talisman, your will, and to a secondary degree your personal emanation, can impregnate a suitable chosen piece of material with lasting power. You can set up in it a 'field' or charge of a particular type of force. But the material to receive this should be new or virgin, although used material can be cleaned and purified. The type of material will affect the permanency of the result. Parchment is more enduring than paper and has other advantages; the nobler metals such as platinum, gold, silver, and even nickel, are less absorptive of gross vibrations; while gem stones, containing the most highly developed mineral life, can sing the same vibrational song over thousands of years.

On the other hand, for a temporary purpose, you can make an effective talisman for a friend from a short length of new cord. Holding it, you make a loose knot, and then concentrate with all the intensity you possess on the quality you are to give. When you feel supremely charged, picture that charge pouring down your arms and concentrating in the knot as you pull it tight with a fierce jerk. Make seven knots like this and you have your talisman.

Supposing you wish to give a ring or jewel for a talismanic purpose, the technique is to visualize a sheet of tense etheric matter between the curved forefinger and thumb of your left hand and, holding the object in your right hand, pass it through the web several times with the intent that all past 'magnetism' be combed out. The object can then be made potent by a process of tension and discharge into it, somewhat similar to the knotting procedure just described. All authorities agree that many types of talisman are better enclosed in silk, and not exposed to the gaze of the inquisitive.

If you acquire a talisman from someone else or buy it in a store, you need to be more aware of how to work with it. Your talisman may have been in contact with a negative force even if it is meant for positive use. This may not cancel it, but it will weaken its power. Prior to activating the talisman, place it in direct sunlight for seven days, this will cancel the negative influences.

VARIOUS METHODS OF CONSECRATION

DIRECT. Hold the object in your hands for as long as you can keep the focus of your purpose on it. Do this for several days. Each morning and each night.

TRANSFERENCE is a simple but powerful method of consecration. You take the object you want to consecrate and place it with other objects that already have the correct energy for the same purpose. You can place it in a covered bowl when working on money. Add a gold piece of jewelry, a silver quarter, gems, etc. Leave them together for awhile. You will feel when the energies are carried over (about a month).

FIRE is an ancient rite of consecration. It has force, power and purification energy. Light a white candle. Hold the object above the candle flame by a chain or rope. Focus all your energy on the object and your intent. (This rite is for any form of money, gambling, legality.)

Repeat three times:

(Say the name of your Divine Power - such as God)
Through your power I ask that it be done.
Let the power of Sachiel,
The powers of Jupiter,
Flow into this talisman (or amulet - specify which),
For the purpose of (specify which purpose),
When I wear this talisman/amulet (specify),
The planets, the earth
And I are one.
This by heaven and earth are done.

WATER. Place the amulet/talisman in your hands, palms together as if in prayer. Submerge your hands and object in the water. Focus all your energy into the object. Call on Divine Power to activate it for your one purpose. Visualize White Light flowing from above your head, down your crown chakra, down your arms, into your hands and into the object. When you feel that you are finished, simply remove it from the water and let it air dry. Your energy flow will charge it much as a battery. The wearer's thoughts are constantly turning towards the talismanic object and picturing its purpose or quality. If it has been impregnated by the act of a powerful will, when one who has faith concentrates his thought upon the talisman, he draws from it a strong suggestion which his own will-power reinforces. Even where there is no 'magnetic charge', the wearer's belief quickly builds up a charge which is effective at subconscious levels.

AIR. Burn the incense of your choice. Hold the object over the smoke from the incense by a rope or chain. Focus your intent. Repeat three times:

By the Power of (your Deity),
By the aid of Nitika,
Let the forces and power,
Flow into this talisman/amulet (specify which),
For wealth (or name financial purpose. Ex; to gamble),
And as this talisman/amulet (specify),
Strong will be,
Now is consecrated unto me,
And as my will, so shall it be.

EARTH. Place the talisman you are charging along with objects of similar purpose (as described above) into a clay flower pot. Fill the vase Fill the pot with fresh soil and the transference of energy will begin. Leave this untouched, for financial gain, for ten days. Take the talisman out and wear or carry it.

After a talisman has been consecrated it should be protected. It should never be handled or even seen by anyone other than its owner. Negative energies can easily be picked up and diminish the powerful charge that the charm inherited through consecration. Keep it in a clean safe place and the same talisman can be used over and over again, as long as it is always called upon for its original intent.

There are many ways to use these seals, and the most effective varies depending upon the type of ritual you can perform with comfort, ease, and confidence.

A simple method for using any of the talisman shown in this book is as follows:

1. Use a fresh sheet of parchment paper and Dove' Blood ink. Trace the seal you are interested in using onto the parchment.

2. On the back side of your parchment, write an explanation of what you wish to accomplish. Be specific and be reasonable. Ask for what you need at that particular time. Know that you are justified in asking for it, and have confidence that God wants you to achieve.

3. Anoint each corner of your seal with an oil appropriate to your intent (Money Drawing, Casino Jackpot etc.)

4. Place your seal in a small flannel sack (the most appropriate color for financial gain is green), along with it place any other object of similar purpose. Anoint the bag with the oil and carry it with you each day until your goal has been accomplished.

Other ritual methods include the use of candles, incense, oils, herbs and powders. The effectiveness of your ritual depends mainly on your confidence and diligence.

MONEY ATTRACTION RUNE

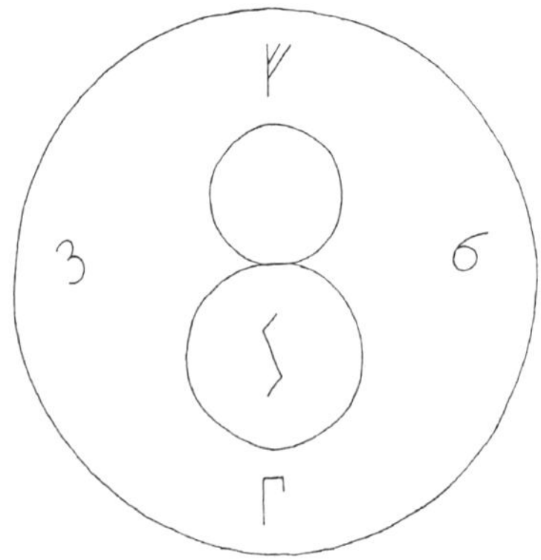

Focus on your intent as you do the following:

Trace the runes Dove's Blood ink.

Trace the other symbols within the circle in green. Also trace the circle itself in green.

Now consecrate this talisman according to your chosen formula.

PROSPERITY DRAWING SIGIL RUNE

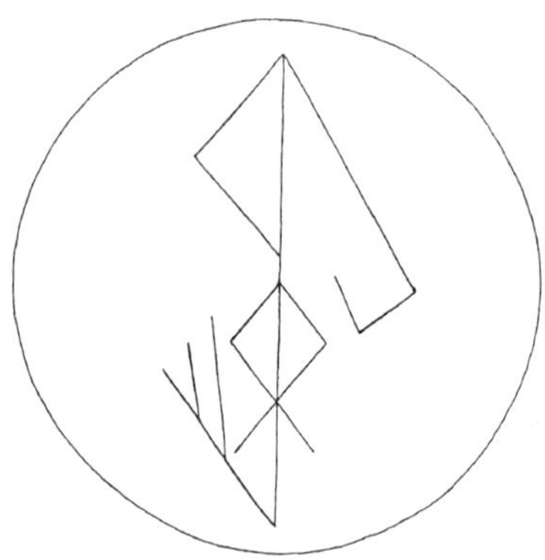

Focus on your intent.

Trace the symbol within the circle in Dove's Blood ink.

Hold it in your hand and focus the intent as long as you are able to.

Now use the method you would feel best with to consecrate it.

RUNIC TALISMAN FOR HAPPINESS, ABUNDANCE, PROSPERITY MAGNET

Focus on your intent.

Trace the pyramid within the circle in black.

Trace all other symbols in bright red.

Consecrate the talisman with the method of your choice.

THE ISLAMIC WEALTH TALISMAN

To be carried or worn for wealth and prosperity and good fortune. It is said, "Prosperous are the believers". It consists of a sickle-shaped moon with a five pointed star drawn within the open part of the sickle on the right side.

TABLE OF JUPITER

Brings good luck, fortune, money, good judgment, long distance travel, business increase, legal matters. Protects against accidents. Causes sympathy in others.

Make a square with three lines running down and three across in the box. You now have sixteen squares. Fill in the numbers as indicated.

4	14	15	1
9	7	6	12
5	11	10	8
16	2	3	13

The total of the numbers is 136. Jupiter's Intelligence is Yophiel (136). The numbers added diagonally and in the horizontal and vertical columns equal 34. The 34 in Hebrew equates to the word for tin. So this talisman should be made on tin on Thursday, which relates to Jupiter.

BRING GAMBLING LUCK

Reproduce (include all the details, but you need not be perfect) this talisman with Dove's Blood ink on parchment paper and tie it to your left forearm with white ribbon while you play. Touch it with your right hand before you begin to gamble. No one else should be aware of your advantage.

BRING CUSTOMERS

The Seal of Schemforas from the 6th & 7th Books of Moses. Reproduce this image on parchment paper. Anoint it with Better Business oil and leave it under a brown candle as it burns. When the candle is done burn the seal and throw the ashes into the wind. Customers will soon come. You can anoint another Seal of Schemaforas with Success oil and sprinkle it wth Allspice. Place it in your cash register or safe.

LUCK WHEN GAMBLING

The Seal of Fortune from the 6th & 7th Books of Moses. Write your wish on the back of the seal, anoint each corner with Lucky Gambler oil and keep it in your wallet with your money.

MONEY DRAWING SEAL

The Seal of Mercury from the 6th & 7th Books of Moses can be used to help draw money for a special need. Reproduce the image on parchment paper, write your special request on the back and anoint the seal each day with Money Drawing oil. Be confident that as you pray, you are bringing about the results you hope for.

FAST LUCK SEAL

The Seal of Good Luck from the 6th & 7th Books of Moses can be used to help bring goog luck in a hurry. Reproduce the image on parchment paper, write your special request on the back and anoint the seal each day with Fast Luck oil.

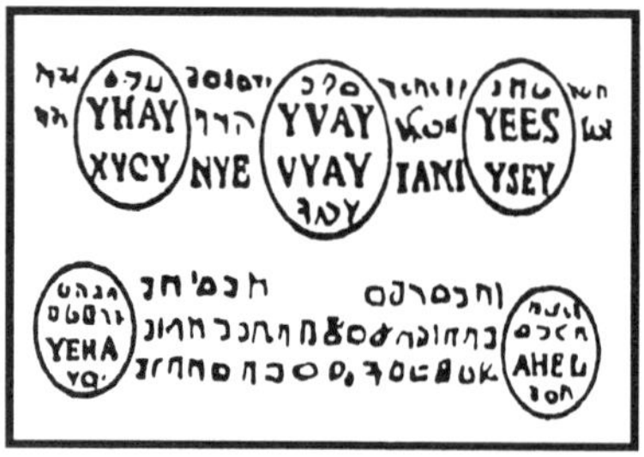

LUCKY LOTTERY SEAL

The Seal of Saturn from the 6th & 7th Books of Moses is said to attract favorable vibrations when participating in any game of chance. Reproduce the image on parchment paper, anoint it and your lottery ticket with Lucky Lottery oil and keep them together until the winning numbers are drawn.

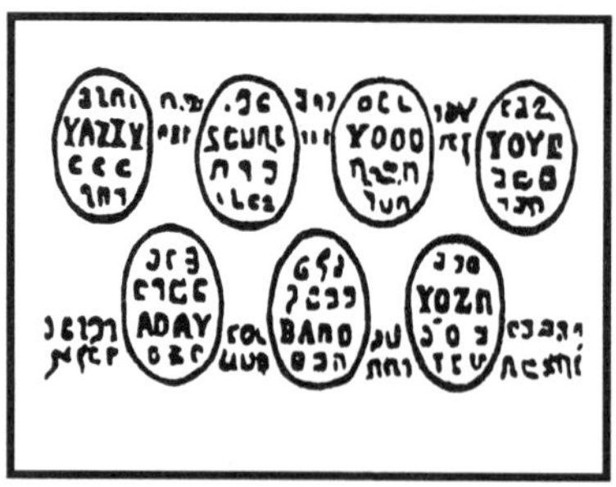

ATTRACT WEALTH & LIFE'S GOOD BLESSINGS

Anoint the Seal of the Sun from the 6th & 7th Books of Moses with Easy Life oil to attract the best things life has to offer. Always carry it with you.

GOOD LUCK & FORTUNE

This Gnostic seal picturing a dove and cornucopia is said to bring health wealth and happiness.

CHU HUA

This Chinese magical seal of the chrysanthemum traditionally attracts an easy life. Wear it to attract Wealth, Health & Happiness

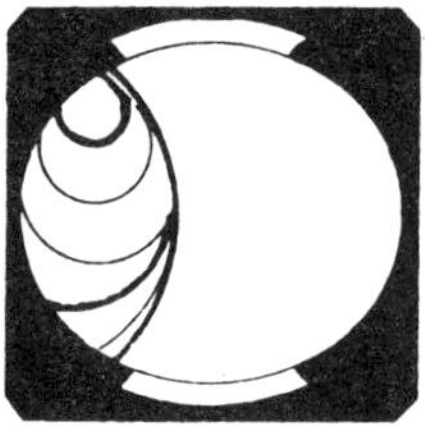

JAPANESE SYMBOL FOR GOOD LUCK

JAPANESE SYMBOL FOR GAMBLING LUCK

ETHIOPIAN GOOD LUCK CHARM

CHINESE DRAGON SEAL FOR GOOD FORTUNE

ST. ANTHONY SEAL FOR LUCK

TALISMAN FOR BUSINESS

This Egyptian glyph resembles the number four. It is used for business success. The hieroglyph should be cast in gold and worn on a chain. The glyph means "to be powerful".

SUCCESS

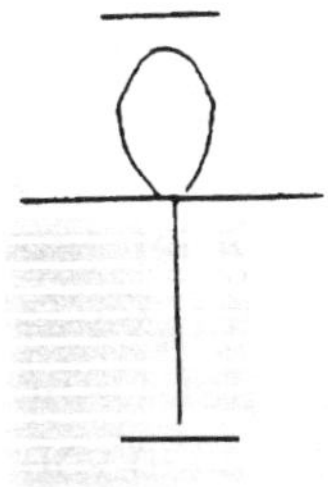

Meant to be made on a piece of long lasting material such as silver or stone. Then it should be worn on the body.

FORTUNE

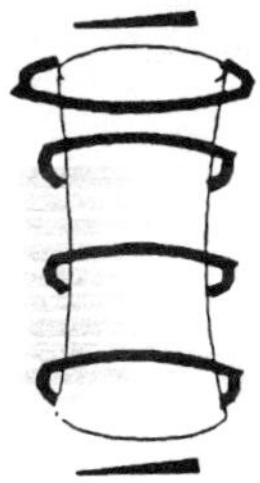

Write this symbol on parchment paper. Fold it in half and carry it in your wallet.

SUCCESS TALISMAN

Draw this glyph on a solid object such as silver. Carry it or wear it.

FORTUNE OF THE ELVES

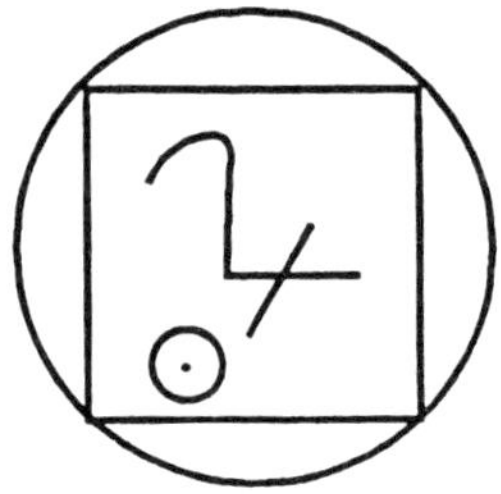

Form the following symbols on tin:
As always, focus on your intent.

THE SQUARE OF ESAUE

This is another well known formula used to gain material and other wealth. Recreate the image below. You need to use a pin to prick your left hand, then, using your own blood as ink, draw onto parchment. Visualize exactly what you want while you are writing these letters. Anoint the parchment daily with any Money Drawing oil, place it in your wallet and carry it with you at all times.

E	S	A	U	E
S				S
A				A
U				U
E	S	A	U	E

FAST MONEY

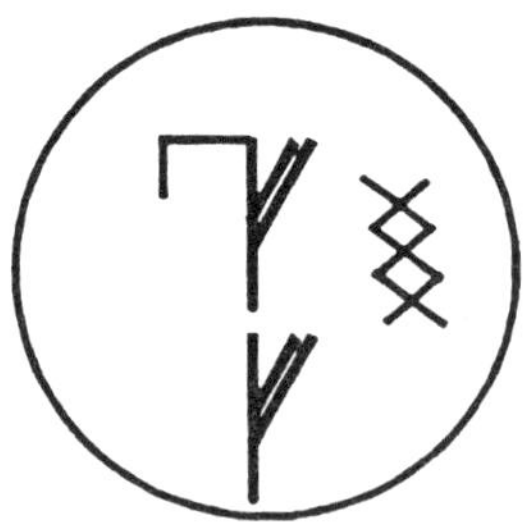

Make this on a Thursday on the 9th, 18th or 27th of the month.Draw the following runes on platinum: Carry or wear it constantly.

CONSECRATION OF RING FOR WEALTH

Use a ring made of any metal, it does not need to be expensive or elaborate. Place the ring on a rope or chain, and place over the flame of a green candle. Focus your energy and that of the flame going into the ring. Say:

As the flames
Reach higher and higher,
This ring attracts wealth.
This is my desire.

And as we will,
So shall it be,
Of earth and air,
Of sun and sea!

It is said that this ring will bring wealth to you if worn every day.

TALISMAN TO GAIN RICHES

This formula is one of the more well known. You need a gold chain. On this place seven gold rings (they can be very inexpensive) Consecrate for wealth as described above and carry it or wear it at all times.

RAINBOW TALISMAN

Take the colors gold, green, lavender, silver and orange from pieces of material. Fold them over a silver quarter that was placed in the center so the silver does not show. Place these in a purple pouch. Hold the pouch with its contents and focus your intent (to attract finance, new job, any goal which deals with money) in your palms. Anoint daily with the oil appropriate to your goal and carry at all times.

MONEY ATTRACTION

Light three candles placed next to each other three inches apart; the middle candle the color green, the two outside candles being white. Hold the object (a ring, talisman, coin, stone, etc.) that you want to energize over the middle flame by a rope, chain or string. Focus on what you want and feel the energy from your hands flow into the object as you repeat:

By the Power of God,
By ten times ten,
This (name the object, such as stone)
now a magnet shall be,
To attract money and wealth,
Be consecrated now unto me.

Partners now in growth we'll be,
And as my will, so mote it be!

Author's Note: I use the number ten very frequently since in the Kabbalah the number becomes the symbol for wealth. When you multiply ten times ten, it equals one hundred which equates to happiness. Further, bringing one hundred down to a single digit (one) through numerology, it then equates to will and force.

Also, the source, God, is mentioned to acknowledge, plus force, plus intent among other things. So when I formulate any magick, there is always more involved than meets the eye. The more you do your own, the better you will become. Most of my own formulae in this book took time to develop and time to watch the outcome. Magick is our oldest science. There is always cause and effect.

ANGELIC FORCES

To consecrate any charm with the power of the Angels, perform the following ritual.

Hold the object between your palms. Your hands will be in the same position as when you pray. Visualize your financial intent. Let the flow of white energy come down from above through your crown chakra, down your arms and into your hands. Say:

I call on the angelic forces,
I call now on Zadkiel,
To consecrate this talisman,
For (fill in your desire) .
And as the energies flow between us,
The talisman and I become one,
And so I say, and so shall it be,
From sun to moon, from earth to sea.

THE EAGLE TALISMAN

If you are in a quandary as to what purpose you want financially, simply choose wealth. This covers everything. (Emotional as well as financial wealth.) Find some feathers and stay outside once you have them; begin your work.

Hold the feathers in your right hand and above your head towards the sky. Say the following, as you pour your energy and intent into them:

By the eagle,
That flies on high,
By the air and sky above,
I consecrate these feathers to me,
To do my bidding and bring my needs.

Through mists of time,
Through dark of night,
The eagle brings in,
All I desire.

CHAPTER 4

THE MAGICK OF OF GEMSTONES

Gemstones may be perceived as a primitive tool. They work on a vibrational level. It does not matter if you have a strong belief in their effects or not; regardless of your thoughts, they will work. This is why they are still in use today.

Gemstones need to be within three feet of your physical body to have the outcome you are working on. When the stones are not near, they are still active but they work for the person who is nearest to them. Stones have always been nature's way of aiding us. You can attract positive situations into your life or use the stones to repel negative situations.

Due to their vibration level, numerous psychics are able to utilize stones for readings to gain information concerning the past, present and the future. They can also be read psychically to acquire information about land and weather changes. Stones are connected to earth energy. Since they are one with and part of the earth, they are also considered valuable. Some were used in the barter system denoting value being placed on them. Our money system also includes gold, silver and other valued minerals.

There have been a number of stone worshiping cults, such as in Hellenic Greece, Thessaly and Crete. Some cultures considered certain stones as Gods due to the qualities of the stone. They were given the attributes of strength, stability, indestructibility. These gave people the feeling of protection and psychic skills were aided by the stones.

Carved figures are still a focus point in varied cultures. The Stone of Fail is located in Dublin, Ireland. This stone was said to scream during the coronation of a king if he was not right for the people. In Egypt, the Lapis Lazuli stone was considered a prized stone. It was utilized to aid in making love, to bring down the Jupiter radiations to this planet, to heighten psychic abilities and to have strong magickal powers.

Stones are also connected to the element off air since both earth and air share the quality of being indestructible, the substance of air being the vital life force. These two elements of air and earth are contained in the human body thus making them compatible. Their vibrations merge together. Among other ways to utilize this force is to heighten psychic skills, healing abilities, luck and stabilizing energies.

CLEANSING

Prior to wearing or putting a stone to work, make sure you cleanse the stone to cancel any negative energy attached to them. The influences of stones are varied depending on each person's vibration. You do not want to work with a stone that may have been handled numerous times by a negative person before you owned it. That does not mean it was consciously done. Look at all the people who may have come into contact with your stone. Some person mined it, a postal service transported it and a store owner who may have a pessimistic attitude on life touched it. You do not need these influences. The cleansing process is very simple. Place the stones in a bowl or dish of water. Add a little salt and leave them in direct sunlight for three days. They do not have to be outside. They can be in direct light on a table in your kitchen. Do not let others touch or handle the stone once you start working with it.

Negative people can cancel what you are working on or tone it down. After three days have passed, your stones possess their true vibratory influences.

Each stone carries more than one vibrational influence. They can be used for more than one purpose. Each stone also has a color. If you are uncertain what the purpose of a specific stone is when you look at it, go by the color. The following chart shows the significance of a particular color stone with regard to its financial properties.

Green	money
Orange	prosperity, luck
Brown	land (real estate, etc.), legal matters
Yellow	clear ideas of concepts to make money, happiness, generosity, legal dealings
Purple	luck, spirituality
Turquoise	luck, protection
White	luck, protection, optimism
Gold	prosperity, success

When beginning to carry a stone or work with one, the best days to start are Sunday, Thursday and Saturday, the best of the three being Thursday. The planetary influences are the Sun, Jupiter and Saturn.

I recommend that if you wear jewelry, consecrate that which you wear frequently and feel comfortable with. However, I would not consecrate a ring for a specific purpose if it belonged to my grandmother. Think about how you will use it later, how often you wear it, if it is something a friend or your son or daughter borrows occasionally. If you feel especially good about a particular stone or are drawn to one, utilize it. It was meant to be yours.

Look at all the contributing factors. Decide what object you want as a talisman or amulet. Decide on your intent. Formulate a new ritual if you would like or pick one. Remember to cleanse the object first.

Now is the time for Enlightenment! Now is the time to begin. Now you are ready to start on the road to manifesting your success.

LEGACY

In Persia it is believed that any Agate utilized as a talisman or amulet will bring fortune in a legacy (will not cause a problem, only if the situation was to come up, then the wearer would be the friend/ relative to gain).

SPECULATIONS

The Assyrians believed that a talisman/amulet made from the gemstone called a Cat's Eye would increase mental ability and fortune in speculations, whether in business or gambling. It is best to wear the Cat's Eye around the neck.

SECRET OF THE DIAMOND

The diamond was not always looked upon favorably. It was different from other stones and seemed to have negative stories or very positive stories, stories of death or stories of wealth.

To bring fortune and strength, the stone should be cut so it has six corners. Of all the cuts of stones, this is the most fortunate. One of the reasons is that the six vibration relates to the six pointed star used by occultists to represent earth, from which all material things come.

VICTORY

Consecrate a Black Agate. This stone has a natural vibration attracting victory and prosperity.

A Brown Agate should be consecrated for wealth.

MONEY ABILITY

Consecrate aluminum for the purpose of acquiring the ability to make money and mental alertness. The correlation being that aluminum is flexible and your mind needs to also be flexible. This would work especially well for those born under the sign of Aquarius, Virgo or Gemini.

WISHES

Zircon is known as the Wishing Stone. Among other results, if consecrated for money and power, this can be a highly attractive force in your life.

PROSPERITY

Soak a Black Agate in a little salt and water mixture in a bowl under your bed for eight nights. Start on the night of the new moon. Then carry it with you at all times. This will help increase prosperity and achieve victory.

GOOD FORTUNE

Wear the stone named Jasper in the color green. You can also place it in your home such as in a planter. It will look decorative next to your plant and people will not question what you are doing. This is a good stone to give as a present.

LIFE LONG WEALTH

Place a Brown Agate under your pillow from the new moon in July until the next new moon in August (one month). Each night as you go to sleep, be in a happy, positive mood and thank the Father for your wealth. When you take the Brown Agate out from underneath your pillow, place it where you keep your money in your house. Leave it there always. This will give you a long, happy and wealthy life.

LUCK

Wear an Amethyst ring when you need luck on your dominant hand (the one you use to write with).

MOBILITY IN BUSINESS

Wear Periodot and Garnet or carry them at all times in your work environment. It will reduce dangerous envy so others will not try to stop or block your opportunities. It also promotes loyalty and picks up financial levels.

INTELLIGENT JUDGMENTS WITH MONEY

I had a client a few years ago who was doing rather well but felt he could be doing much better. He wanted to move up into a management position on his job. He was good at making decisions. However, any time his boss asked for an opinion, my client grew so tense that it showed him as being incapable. This situation grew worse. He knew he had the ability and knew he could do the job better compared to those already in that position, not to mention, making more money does not hurt. We did a psychic reading on it. This brought about his wearing a Turquoise stone at all times - all day, every day.

The Turquoise eased his physical and mental tension (so he could handle himself with confidence) and attracted money to him. Within two months, he had the job he wanted. He no longer needed to carry the stone since it already did its job. He framed it at home with a little note under it that said, "All I need is hidden within this stone". He also gives something back to keep the flow going by giving supportive feedback to those working under him.

So to aid in being calm enough to make positive judgments and attract money, wear the Turquoise stone at all times until your goal is accomplished.

TO IMPROVE BUSINESS

Place a Jasper and Bloodstone together into the back of your cash register. Take another Jasper and Bloodstone and hold these in your hands. Concentrate on your needs, breathe on them, then place them into a green pouch. Carry this pouch with you at all times. Do not tell others about what you are working on. Remember to be honest, optimistic and to respect your customers. They will be aware and keep coming back.

FORTUNATE END IN LAWSUITS

Carry the stones called Hematite, Rhodochrosite and Malachite. Have them with you at all times when you deal with anyone or anything concerning the case, even when you are only on the telephone.

TO GET A BETTER JOB

Carry Lapis Lazuli in an orange bag.

GOOD LUCK

They say that if you wrap a Moonstone in a yellow cloth, it will attract good luck when carried. (If given to someone you love, it will bring the person to you.)

DOUBLE LUCK

At the time of a full moon, perform the following ritual:

1. Light Patchouli Incense.
2. Place the gemstone Tiger's Eye next to it.
3. Focus your intent on the stone as you sprinkle it with Double Luck Powder.
4. When the incense is finished, pick up the stone. Focus on your needs again.
5. Thank Divine Power for your abundance and luck coming in. Know it. Feel it.
6. Carry the stone with you for Double Luck.

SUCCESS AND GOOD FORTUNE

During the month of December, take a Turquoise stone and inscribe this symbol with silver paint. Always keep it with you.

GOOD LUCK IN ANY ENDEAVOR

Lodestones are carried in a pair and placed in a red bag. The purpose is for one to cancel evil and the other to attract good luck. The stones are usually used in their natural state. They are grayish black in color. However, in our modern times, you can also acquire them in colors (red for love, white for protection against negative forces). For our purpose you would use gold, silver, green or the natural color. These attract money and luck.

The Lodestones are "fed" on every Friday by either adding over them or immersing them in magnetic sand. However, you first need to empty the old sand outside of your home.

ANOTHER LUCKY CHARM

Place the following stones in a white bag and carry within three feet of your body at all times:

Jasper *(green)* • Tiger Eye *(green)* • Jade *(green)*
Turquoise • Apache Tear • Clear Quartz Crystal

EASY LUCK

During a full moon in the month of January, take a piece of silver and a Jade stone to a body of water (an ocean, river, stream or any other form). Hold them submerged for a minute and ask the elemental spirit of the water, named Neska, through God, to come to your aid in enriching your life through gaining wealth.

Thank Neska, then thank God. For it is done. Go home and wear the stones around your neck in a small leather pouch.

TO FULFILL ANY WISH

Soak an uncut Moonstone in fresh (or tap) water with a Quartz Crystal. Do this three days prior to a new moon. Upon the night of the new moon, take it out, place it on a chain (long enough to reach your heart chakra). Wear it at all times (day and night). until the next full moon. During this time, declare what you want (possession, money coming in, etc). Do only one purpose at a time. Say aloud and contemplate the following affirmation as often as you'd like while visualizing what you desire:

> *No opportunity that is mine by Divine Right can be taken from me, blocked or stopped (visualize your desire) by anyone or anything. I now attract to me the right (abundant finance, etc.).*

RITUAL OF SUCCESS

1. Light two white candles on an altar or table.
2. Place an orange candle in the center.
3. Wear something orange.
4. Have the gemstone called Bloodstone on your altar.
5. Burn the herb Alfalfa over charcoal.
6. Say:

> *I invoke the magick to work miracles, as was done by magi before me. Through God and Cosmic Forces, what man can believe, man can manifest. Let these words form power as they are spoken. I conjure this command thus (Fill in your intent.) So Be It!*

Snuff the candles and the incense. Carry the gemstone with you.

HUNGARIAN JINX REMOVING

To cancel negative energy sent by someone not wishing you well financially, place the following items in a yellow bag:

Tiger Eye *(brown)* • Bloodstone
Clear Quartz Crystal • Carnelian

Hold the bag in your hands, focus on sending back ONLY what is sent to you through Divine Power in a Perfect Way. Bless the person (if you do not know who, say "the person") who wishes you not to do well and send the person love. Only positive energy will cancel negative. If you send negative back, you are only feeding it and giving it more power. Keep the bag with you until you feel it has had its desired effect.

MAGYAR PROSPERITY MAGNET

Take a piece of gold and starting on the time of the new moon, place it in a bowl. Pour white wine over the gold until it is covered. Look at the gold and see it as a magnetic force. Visualize all good and all types of money coming to it (such as cash, checks, etc.).

Thank God for all the abundance attracted to you. Know it. Feel it. It will come. Leave it overnight in a place where the moon can shine down upon it. The next morning, take the gold out of the wine and wrap it in a piece of green material. Take the wine and throw it away outside of your home.

Carry the gold wrapped in the green material at all times. Each morning, look at it and focus on financial prosperity increasing and being attracted to it.

MAGYAR MAGICK TO BRING IN CASH

On white paper write the following with black ink;

> *Istenen Keresztül, most jön be minden amit akarok pénzel és töb. Minden nap a pénz töb és töbet nö.*

Fold a dollar bill in fourths and place it in the center. Place the stone called Jade on top of the bill. Next, fold the white paper over both to cover them so they can't be seen. Tie green ribbon or thread around the white paper to keep it sealed. Always keep it with you.

TO INCREASE YOUR WEALTH

Hold the stone called Adventurine in your hand. Close your eyes and relax. Take three to four deep breaths. Open your eyes and focus on the stone. Say:

> *Let the Power of the stars, the Power of the earth,*
> *the Power of the moon, the Power of the sun,*
> *aid me in my quest. When I carry this magick stone,*
> *My money increases and expands.*
> *So do I say and so shall it be.*

Then carry it where others will not see it or touch it. Remember to be honest and have patience as the outcome is guaranteed. After all, God does not make mistakes and as you asked, you were answered.

TO CANCEL MONEY HEX

Keep a Tiger Eye in the middle of a table within easy sight.

TO KEEP MONEY FLOWING

Keep a dish with earth in direct sunlight. Place a Tourmaline stone in the center each night and thank it through Divine Power for the help you are receiving in moving towards money stability and wealth. Each morning put it in your pocket (wallet, etc.) to carry with you all day.

Find a way to help someone from your heart each day, even if it is just a small favor, such as, if the person needs a ride somewhere or if one dollar for a cup of coffee is needed. Bless what you do and know it is coming back in a way that *you* need.

GOLD TO GOLD

Pyrite is the stone also known as Fools Gold. When the Gold Rush came in the United States, many people were mislead by this stone. They thought the Pyrite was real gold and assumed they had hit a streak of luck. This was not the case. Some did discover that by carrying pyrite they did well financially. *"Like attracts like"* has been known and put to work in Voodoo for centuries. The vibration of this stone will attract gold to you and its equivalent. Carry Pyrite in a green charm bag anoint it each day with Money Drawing oil.

POWER OF INDIA

Place the following stones in a white bag then tie it with eight knots; *3 Apache Tears, 1 Moss Agate, 2 Lodestones.* Sprinkle a few drops of Indian Oil into the palms of your hands. Next, hold the conjure bag between your palms, rub back and forth and focus on luck and power.

SPEEDY MONEY ATTAINMENT

1. Acquire one each of the following:

   Adventurine • Clear Quartz Crystal • Tiger's Eye

2. Anoint each gem and crystal with Van Van Oil after smudging them with Sage Incense.

3. Place the stones in a leather bag and add a pinch each of these herbs:

   Mullein • Sage • Peppermint
   Rosemary • Chamomile

4. Carry the pouch with you. It is said that money will soon come you way.

CHANGE YOUR LUCK

1. Anoint a green candle with Lucky Prophet Oil.

2. Place a parchment paper under your candle with your desire.

3. Place the stone called a Clear Quartz Crystal on the top of the candle prior to lighting it.

4. Light the candle and when it is burned to the bottom, take the stone out and carry it.

CHAPTER 5

THE POWER OF HERBS, ROOTS AND FLOWERS

Herbs, roots and bark have been employed since ancient times by Druids, Romans, Egyptians and diverse unknown cultures, priests and sorcerers down through the ages. The knowledge passed through sects and ones of power. There exist a number of books available on medical or medicinal herbal uses. There are also a number of books on describing the power of herbs for occult use. Authors of occult and other books do not always give the same uses for an herb; however, that is only due to its versatility. Mainly in dealing with the occult, herbs are utilized to cast spells. They vibrate to certain planets, angels, days and hours.

At times herbs are used as extracts, in teas or for baths. Herbs are sometimes worn as talismans, buried, sprinkled and thrown to the winds. They are also used as needed for divergent purposes such as protecting or hexing, to make wishes come true, to attract or hold love, money, power or control. Any intention you may conceive can be helped one way or another with an herb. Herbs, though not necessarily understood by all, have been so employed for thousands of centuries. Nothing that stays with us such a length of time can be said to not work when properly used or to be only harmful. The more regard we pay towards out pasts, the more we may control and enliven our futures.

COLORING HERBS

Native Americans and various tribes in other countries have used herbs to make colors. Utilize this valuable information to add to money and various prosperity formulae.

Sage	**Green**	Money and material success
Walnut Hulls	**Brown**	Material gain and court cases
Golden Seal	**Yellow**	Clarity and sudden changes
Henna Leaves	**Yellow**	Clarity and sudden changes
Sumac Leaves	**Brown**	Material gain and court cases

MONEY MASTERY

1. Buy an uncut lemon making sure that there aren't any scratches on the surface.
2. Hang the lemon up at your place of business or in your home.
3. Do not cut the lemon anywhere. Hang it up by wrapping string around it or a coat hanger or any other form you can think of to make certain it is not on a flat surface.

Money will come in, or the opportunity to make money, within seven days. I hang mine up and tell people that it is an air freshener.

EGYPTIAN ATTRACTION

Some authorities say that the onion was worshipped in Egypt in various locales. The onion comes under the element of fire and is connected with the female deity called Isis. Take the skin of the onion. It should be burned in a fireplace or stove along with any peelings. This will attract riches. Do not throw them on the ground as that will cancel riches coming to your home.

ANTI-THEFT

Burn Khus-Khus *(Vertivert)* with a protection incense such as High John. It will keep theft from your door.

Khus-Khus will also heighten business when placed in your cash register. This very versatile herb can be added to any money or luck mixture.

THE ALLURE OF GOLD

Like attracts like, so carry the stone called Pyrite in a yellow pouch. Add three herbs *Golden Seal, Sage, Henna* and the following two seals:

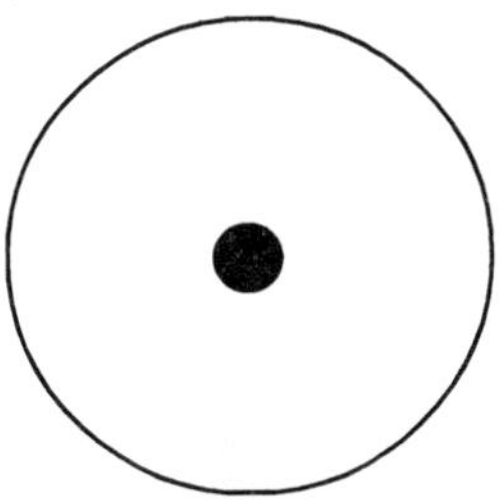

Seal of the Sun

Seal of Good Fortune

Anoint the pouch with Almond Oil. Carry it with you.

Next, make another exactly like the first and place this next to the phone. To attract continuous business, leave it there.

SHAMAN'S LUCKY MONEY DRAWING POUCH

Place the following ingredients leather pouch and carry it with you at all times:

1 Jasper stone (green)
1 green feather
Mullein
Cloves
Rosemary
Irish Moss
Chamomile
Bayberry
Cinnamon

LUCKY CHARMS

Carry individually or together as charms:

Buckeye
Cedar
Nutmeg
Clove
Orris Root
Pecan
Almond
Oat
Cashew
Jezebel Root

ASIAN LUCK

In Asia some carry Holy Sandalwood to attract luck. It can also be burned as incense for this purpose.

GOOD LUCK

Wear Tonka Beans and Grains of Paradise in a pouch around your neck.

MOJO POWER

In a green mojo bag, carry Lavender and add 1 quarter, 1 dime, 1 nickel, 1 penny.

FAST MONEY

Place the following items in a red pouch:

2 Lodestones
Horse Chestnut
Snapdragon
Fern
Woodruff

Anoint the pouch and its contents with Success Oil and Almond Oil. Wrap money around the bag and carry it.

MONEY DRAWING

On a Thursday, place the following items in a green bag:

Fenugreek
Orris Root
Chamomile
Seal of Prosperity
Jade stone
Money Drawing Powder
Something personal (hair, etc.)

Anoint the bag with Money Drawing Oil. Anoint a green seven-day candle with Money Drawing oil, burn one knob each day. While the candle burns anoint the bag with the same oil, contemplate on your desire as you do so.

JOB HOLDING

1. Place the following items in a red bag:

   High John Root
   Devil's Shoestring Root
   (tie a white thread around this root)
   Lucky Hand Root
   Red Clover
   Chamomile
   2 Tonka Beans
   Star of Anise
   Seal for Release from Want

2. Once a week, dress the bag with Success Oil

3. Bathe each day for 1 week in Money Drawing Salts, and dust your body with Success Powder upon leaving your home.

4. As you take your bath each day burn 1 knob of a green 7-knob candle that has been anointed with Success Oil. Try not to skip a day.

TO WIN IN COURT

Wear something pink when entering the court. The color needs to be visual to others. Carry a Devil's Shoestring Root and have faith that the verdict will be positive.

TO BRING MONEY

Carry Sandalwood and charcoal.

LUCK WITH PROPERTY

Bury Dandelions under the northwest house corner. It will also attract luck to those inside.

FOREST RITUAL

During a new moon, do this ritual to gain financial increase.

1. Find an oak tree and dig a small hole at the roots on the north side of the tree. Do not disturb the roots, dig between or next to them.

2. Into the hole place a piece of white paer on which you've written your intention.

3. On top of the paper sprinkle the following herbs:

Basil	*Marjoram*
Allspice	*2 Grapes or leaves*
Cowslip	*Lucky Hand*
Rice	

4. Cover the hole with the dirt. While you are covering it say:

   Through Divine Power,
   Through Hathor and Dionysus,
   I ask the Spirit of the Tree,
   The Earth and the Spirits of Nature,
   To manifest for me my desires.
   I desire (fill in your needs).

5. Then stand up, turn your back to the tree and walk away. Do not look back. Know that your needs will be fulfilled.

DAME FORTUNE

1. In an area with Pine trees, dig a small hole at the base do not disturb the roots.

2. Place into it a parchment paper with your name and your intent. Add:

Aloe	*Violet*
Daffodil	*Bamboo*
7 Job's Tears	*Strawberry (fruit or leaves)*
Holly	

3. Sprinkle over it Cinnamon Oil.

4. Focus on your intent while you cover the hole. Walk away and do not look back. Fortune shall come your way.

HOLLYHOCK SPELL

You need the seeds from the Hollyhock, a few new, a few older and from the ground. Place them on white paper. Fold the paper. Next to a northern wall, bury it with one silver coin, one copper coin and any other coin. Add Orris Root and more Hollyhock. Do this in the Fall. By the Spring you will see the growth of finance.

MONEY ATTRACTION TO YOUR HOME

Boil as an infusion some Fenugreek seeds.
Wash the floors in all the rooms of your home.
Place some seeds in your wallet or purse.
Do this once a week.

SECURE YOUR INCOME

Stuff the following herbs into a green doll:

Comfrey — *Chamomile Flowers*
Queen's Root — *Lemon Rind*

On a piece of parchment paper write the income you want each month or year. Also write the following verse:

I seek the aid of Divine Power,
I will use the money wisely,
And will put some back to helping others.
Grant the amount of ($ fill in $),
To me through Divine Right,
Through Attis, Astarte, Cybele.
So Be It.

Sign your name. Place it inside the doll. Sew the doll back up with white thread. Anoint the doll with Success Oil and Holy Oil. Place it under your mattress.

GOOD LUCK SPELL

In a pot boil 12 cups of water containing:

2 Tablespoons Chamomile Flowers
2 Tablespoons Grains of Paradise
1 Tablespoon Vetivert
1 slice of Pineapple
1/2 of an Orange

Allow to boil for 20 minutes. After it has cooled pour some of the mixture over your hands and sprinkle it throughout your home.

MERLIN'S FORCE

Boil in an iron pot 12 cups of water and add the following herbs:

Jasmine
Oak
Lavender
Marigold
One green stone

When done, wash hands in the water when it cools down. Sprinkle the rest around your premises. Carry the stone with you.

POPPY SPELL

Dress a one dollar bill with Poppy Oil. Start at the upper right corner and go clockwise. Do not break contact. Next, fold it so the pyramid is showing and keep it in your wallet.

TO FIND MONEY

In a green mojo bag, place some Gold Magnetic Sand and Smartweed. Add the Seal of Treasure. Also add the Highest Seal of Good Fortune. Anoint the mojo bag with Jupiter Oil. Carry it next to your wallet.

LEGALITIES

For a better outcome to a court case, place Buckthorn, Hickory and Marigold in a yellow pouch and keep it with you at all times through the final verdict.

PLANT POWER

Sprinkle around the base of a 7-day green candle some Alfalfa, Clover and Snapdragon. Buy a Snapdragon plant and keep it in your home.

BUCKTHORN WISH

The old ones say that you will see elves if you dance by the light of the full moon in a circle made of Buckthorn. If you carry the Buckthorn, it is an aid in legal matters, prosperity and granting wishes.

CIRCLE OF THE ELVES

Blend together:

Pine	*Golden Seal*
Fenugreek	*Hops*
Vetivert	*Dill*
Ginger	

In a clearing near trees or bushes, sprinkle the blend in a small circle in front of you. Say in a loud voice (for the elves to hear), what your request is. Then thank the Spirits of Nature for their aid.

LUCKY PINEAPPLE SPELL

The dried peel and dried flesh are carried to attract luck and money. They can also be added to other money mixtures.

If you add the dried pineapple (you can place it in cloth) to bath water, it attracts luck to the person. Also add a little of the juice.

CARVED BAMBOO

On a piece of bamboo, carve your wish and bury it.

If you carve the pentagram upon the bamboo, bury it near your home for protection and luck. Place above your door to bring luck in.

MONEY WISHING SPELL

Take some Grains of Paradise (also known as African Pepper) in your hands. Focus on one wish. Throw a little in each direction beginning to the North to the winds. Move clockwise.

These grains are also for luck, money, lust and love. You can add them to any blend for these intents.

ALTAR OF ABUNDANCE

Use a white altar cloth. Place a deep blue square on it. Next place a smaller square of yellow or orange cloth on top.

Place the following objects anywhere on the cloth:

1 green candle (anoint with Vervain Oil)
1 white candle (anoint with Wisteria Oil)
1 ear of corn
some Linden
some Sage
Jasmine Incense

Make your petition through God and through the deity called Hina.

VENUSIAN LUCK

The Tonka Beans are connected to the planet Venus and the element of water. mTo manifest a wish, hold the beans in your hand and focus on your petition, Then toss them into running water.

To attract money, wear Tonka Beans in a green pouch around your neck.

CLAIM TO RICHES

The Fern is a well-known wealth and luck drawing plant. It can be added to any money drawing blend. Keep the plant in your home to protect from ever going broke. Wear some in a green pouch on a string around your neck to attract money. Rub it (or Mint leaves) on and inside your wallet then carry it.

WREATH OF PROSPERITY

Make a wreath from Pine and Oak leaves. Place (you can use white thread to tie objects on) the following on the wreath:

Sea Salt (can be in a pouch)
Lodestones
Pine Nuts
Aloe
A religious symbol (or more than one)

Hang this on or above your door. It will attract prosperity and protection to your home.

KANALOA'S PROSPERITY

This Hawaiian deity connects to the planet Venus and the plant called Banana. It is a highly respected tree in magickal use, among other reasons, because in many rituals it is used to represent the Higher Forces. Both the Forces and the Banana Flowers are hermaphroditic. All parts of this tree (fruit, flowers, etc.) are used to add to money and prosperity rituals. Any part can be dried and carried on your body. It is said to be very powerful.

HAND OF POWER

The Hand of Power is another name for the Lucky Hand. It is a root utilized frequently in magick. It can be used alone or added to any pouch or purpose dealing with success and luck.

- It is carried to have positive employment.
- If you want money, carry it in your wallet.
- For protection, wear it around your neck and one in your shoe.

MUMMY'S FERN

Also known as the Rose of Jericho, when you place the plant into water, it comes to life and opens up and turns green. Place it in a bowl of water with some change (any coins will do), a Jasper, a Clear Quartz Crystal and leave it. Add water when needed or change the water. Ask for Divine aid to increase your wealth.

When you leave it out of the water, it will dry back up into a round sphere to be reused at a later date.

ENCHANTING FORMULA

1. Place two Lodestones in a green pouch.
2. Add a Patchouli herb and a dried orange and lemon rind.
3. Tie the pouch with white string and seven knots.
4. Place this where it will not be touched.
5. Leave it for seven days. The next day, start to carry it.
6. Sew some Alfalfa herb in the hem of your clothing.
7. Money will come to you.

CHAPTER 6

LIGHT MAGICK WITH CANDLES

There are countless authorities and traditions which attempt to tell you precisely what to do in each type of candle-burning ritual or "spell," but few which attempt to explain the reasons why it must be just so. The actual reason is because that is what works best for them - but does it mean anything to you?

The one basic simple fact we can feel sure of is that the act of burning candles does indeed cause an altered state of awareness, producing changes in circumstances. Think of the millions of men and women who have been persuaded and seduced, or extracted promises and proposals, concluded business deals, patched up squabbles, and resolved differences of opinion in the glowing magic of a candlelight supper. And many a birthday wish has come true when all the candles were blown out!

It doesn't matter what your religion is. You really don't have to be religious (or anti-religious) at all. Candle burning is a Psychic and Psychological experience, and may compliment your particular faith by arranging your rituals to blend into it. Nevertheless, you need not do anything which you feel is inharmonious with your personal beliefs, as there are countless alternatives.

The most important thing is that you understand what you are doing, and to create and develop your own techniques and rituals which well surely bring you the results you desire.

When the novice enters the local supply shop he is faced with a myriad of strange looking candles of different sizes, shapes and colors-some of them downright frightening in appearance! It is no wonder that the majority of "Good Christians" consider the "entire" Art as "the work of the devil" - Black Magic Voodoo.

However, when you understand what each of these mysterious objects is intended to represent and how it is used, you will realize that a red nude figure, or a black or green "devil" may be just as innocent as a pink birthday candle - and the skull candles are not simply halloween decorations.

There are no firm rules as to what must be said or done in each case in order to effect a successful candle spell. It must mean something to the operator performing it. Some may achieve results by burning a single candle with a purpose firmly in mind.

Others may do better with an elaborate ceremony, surrounded by symbols and vested in eloquent robes. It can be as simple or as complicated as you wish to make it. The important thing is to pour a part of yourself into each spell. You will eventually learn to create your own chants, movements, dramatizations, and rituals.

THE SIGNIFICANCE OF COLOR

The color of the candle used correlates with the vibrational influence. When you think of money you automatically think of green. If you wish to attract love into your life, the first color you would associate love with would be red. Using the correct color of what you are working on manifesting into your life aids on the vibration level.

Red: Color of life, will power. Burned for love, sex appeal, sexuality, courage, health, strength, increasing energy levels. Attracts women.

Pink: Color of affection and service, truthfulness. Burned for love, honor, gentleness and Spiritual awakening, diplomacy, success, health.

Red & Pink: Attract men.

Orange: Color of joy and enthusiasm, prosperity, energy, courage, adaptability. Burned to influence friendships, stimulation, increase mental strength.

Yellow: Color of intellect and imagination, invokes spirits, creative, action, cheerfulness, joy, charm, warmth and strength.

Blue: Color of balance and abundance. Burned for stability, youthfulness, attracts money, success, luck, healing, fertility, good crops, health, cooperation and generosity.

Brown: Color of practicality and solidarity, earthly planes, legal and material levels. Burned for slowing down mental process, balance, thrift, telepathic communication.

Black: Color of negativity and depression, un-hexing. Burned for banishing rituals, remembrance and mourning, protection from evil, shield.

Violet: Color of sentimentality and royalty. Burned for tranquillity and sedation.

Purple: Color of luxury and power. Burned for ambition, wisdom, psychic development, draws in spiritual energy, protection, self-esteem, goal attainment, prestige and spirit contact. (Recommended to burn a white candle also.)

Silver: Color of stability, neutrality. Burned for psychic development, remove evil influence, good conquering evil.

Gold: Color of universal brotherhood. Burned for good health, good fortune, intellect, study, teaching, persuasive, universal love.

White: Color of purity, truth, cleanliness, spirituality. Burned for protection, universal color of power and positive vibration, hope, peace, cleansing of a negative atmosphere

DRESSING THE CANDLE

Candles should be anointed prior to use for vibrational energy for most candle magick. The oil needs to be harmonious thus it will be for the same purpose as your intent. It is extremely important that you cleanse the candle of any negative vibrations it might have absorbed from the many people that have handled it prior to your purchase. This is very simple. To banish negativity, first rub a little baby oil or virgin olive oil into the palms of your hands wipe one hand at a time from the base to the wick of the candle. You're done.

To bless or anoint (and you can use any size candle) for the purpose of your ritual use, starting from the middle of the candle, rub the oil upwards to the tip of the wick. Then starting once again from the middle, rub down to the bottom. Candles have polarity. Top is the "North Pole"; the bottom is the "South Pole".

You do not need to buy a candle at a religious store. It can be from the supermarket. The best are made from bees wax. The rest are paraffin or vegetable oil.

You are now ready to begin your ritual work.

ALTAR OF GOLD

On an altar, place a yellow candle, a gold candle and a green candle. Anoint all three with Success Oil. As the candle burn, also burn Success Incense. Focus on your clearly defined intent.

DOUBLE ACTION

Anoint a Double Action green and black candle with Success Oil. When you light the candle think about your goal and how you will actively take part in achieving it. Let the candle burn itself out.

BUSINESS SUCCESS

Anoint a white 7-day Pull-Out candle with Prosperity Oil. On white paper write what your purpose is concerning business. Place the paper under the candle. Light the candle and focus your intent. Each day for five minutes, focus on the candle flame and what you desire.

WORK IMPROVEMENT

Anoint a green candle with Money Oil. Light it and read Psalm 61 in the Bible. Focus on the words you read. Know that it is done.

FORTUNE

On a piece of white paper, write your intent. Place this under a pink candle after anointing it with Prosperity Oil. Light the candle. Read Psalm 98 in the Bible three times. Focus on the words.

FINANCIAL SUCCESS

To bring in financial success, burn a gold candle anointed with Success Oil. Read Psalm 150 from the Bible three times. Focus on the words.

RELEASE FROM MONEY DIFFICULTIES

Anoint a brown candle with Success Oil. Read Psalms 54 and 71 from the Bible. Use sincere prayer with this. Repeat each day until your result comes in.

QUICK MONEY

Anoint a blue candle with Fast Luck Oil. Read Psalm 81 from the Bible each day until you receive your desires. this ritual can also be used for health to create blessings in the home.

BLACK CAT SPELL

Burn the Black Cat candle. Light it and while you focus on the flame, focus on good luck and money coming to you. Let the candle burn itself out.

MONEY RITUAL FOR LUCK

1. On an altar covered with white cloth, place a square green cloth.

2. Light High John the Conqueror incense.

3. Anoint a Black Cat candle with Wealthy Way oil.

4. Write the amount of money needed on parchment paper. Place it beneath the candle.

5. Burn the Cat candle for seven minutes the first night, eleven minutes the second, seven minutes again on the third night. Alternate each night with the time. Do this until your luck picks up.

SEVEN KNOB CANDLES FOR WISHING

The Seven Knob Candle is also called the "Wish" candle. For luck or money, use a green Seven Knob Candle.

For One Wish: On parchment paper write your wish and place it beneath the candle. Each day burn one knob and focus on your wish.

More Than One Wish: Write a seperate wish on each of seven sheets of parchment paper. Tie or pin one wish to each knob on the candle. Burn one knob each day. As the knob with the wish is burned, the vibration goes out to attract your wish. Anoint the candle with an oil that matches your wish.

WEALTH MAGNET

Anoint a green candle with Wealthy Way oil. Place the Seal of Mercury underneath it. Burn five minutes per day.

INFLUENCE MONEY OPPORTUNITIES

Cover your altar with a white cloth. Place a religious symbol in the center of the altar and in front of it place some Good Luck incense. On the top right and left corners place a white candle anointed with All Purpose oil.

Anoint two green candles with Chinese Luck oil and place them on the bottom right and left corners Light the incense and candles and say this affirmation aloud:

I now attract what is mine
By Divine Right.
I desire (fill in your desire).

Allow the candle to burn themselves out and be confident that money making opportunities will be presenting themselves to you soon.

TO DRAW MONEY

Anoint a green candle with Money Drawing oil while focusing on the outcome you desire. Place the Jezebel Root halfway under the candle. Burn the candle until it is finished. Place the Jezebel Root with the wax still on it into a green conjure bag. Anoint this bag each day with Money Drawing oil and carry it at all times.

ENSURE PROSPERITY

Follow these steps on a daily basis in your home or your place of business until your prosperity starts to come in. Burn an orange candle anointed with Prosperity oil. Around the base of the candle sprinkle and burn Patchouly incense. Sprinkle Sandalwood powder around the premises. Wear the Prosperity oil each day on your wrists and on your third eye (in the middle of your forehead).

ACHIEVE FINANCIAL SUCCESS

Utilize a white, green and pink candle. Anoint each with Almond Oil. Also add Almond Oil to Finance Drawing Incense. Focus on your intent. Do this for seven days.

TO GAIN MONEY

Cover your altar with a white cloth. Place a Bible in the center. On the left bottom corner place a white Crucifix Altar Candle dressed with High Altar Oil. Place a gold candle anointed with Money Drawing oil above it. Place two green candles dressed with Lady Luck oil on the right bottom corner. Read Psalm 41 from the Bible each day until you have accomplished your goal.

ALL GOOD FORTUNE

Burn a green candle anointed with Patchouli Oil. Read Psalms 73 to 83. When you are finished, say a prayer for the purpose you need to manifest. Do this as often as you wish until you have accomplished your goal. Remember always to thank the powers that be for their assistance.

CHAPTER 7

GAMBLING WIZARDY

Games of chance and varied forms of gambling have always been with us. So, of course, there were those who always wanted to increase the odds in their favor. Some people have a natural feel for gambling in one form or another. Others have ways to manifest, to increase their luck. When utilizing methods through the occult, be aware of the way it works. It does not guarantee you will always win. It does heighten the level of luck so you will win more frequently or receive a larger amount of money through the use of whatever the technique is that you decide upon. Luck in anything is being at the right place at the most opportune moment, listening to your instincts and then moving on it. When deciding which formula fits you, consider which one feels right to you, has the ingredients that are available in your area and is designed for your purpose. Create and increase your luck and have fun with it.

LUCKY GAMBLING DAYS

First sprinkle your hands with Fast Luck or Gambling Powder. Next, look up *(next page)* the best day of the week to play according to your astrological sign.ambling on this particular dayshould increase your frequency of "hits".

Your Sign Astrologically	*Your Best Day*
Leo or Capricorn	Monday
Cancer or Taurus	Tuesday
Virgo or Pisces	Wednesday
Libra or Aires	Thursday
Aquarius or Sagittarius	Friday
Scorpio or Gemini	Saturday

OILS FOR LUCK

There are numerous oils to change the vibrations around you to change your luck. Some of these are:

Success
Fast Luck
Money Drawing
Magnet
Cleo May
Lucky John the Conqueror
High John the Conqueror
Anise
Jockey Club
Jinx Removing (with any lucky oil added)
Lucky Planet

Oils can be used to anoint the body, a mojo bag, to consecrate an environment, a candle, a bath and to be blessed and to cancel negativity. People are sensitive to color, smell and touch. The oil changes the vibration to attract or repel situations. The name tells you what type of vibration is being caused by the oil.

MOJO MONEY BAG

In a green bag, carry a small magnetic horseshoe, nutmeg, Seal of Good Luck, a Seal of Fortune, a parchment paper folded twice with your name and a dollar sign and a horseshoe drawn on it. Also add Alfalfa. Sprinkle the mojo bag once a week on your astrologically correct day with Success Oil. Focus on your intent.

GAMBLING LUCK

Carry in your pocket a Black Agate and a Brown Agate. The black for success in games and the brown stone for riches.

EUROPEAN LUCKY CARDS

In Europe, the professional card players use this method. They boil approximately one cup of water with three tablespoons of the herb Chamomile for about 30 minutes, covering the pot while boiling on a lower setting. Then they wait for it to cool down (strain the herbs if you wish so you are only left with the liquid). Next, they wash their hands with the liquid prior to playing cards. For some reason, this method only works well for gambling with cards.

VOODOO OIL

A famous oil used in Voodoo is called *"Has No Hanna Oil"*. You rub this oil on your hands before gambling.

GAMES OF CHANCE

Place a medium to large sized High John Root in a pot of water and bring this to a boil. Wash your hands in this after the water cools before playing game of chance. Wear Money Drawing Oil, Jasmine Oil, Sandalwood Oil, Gambler's Oil or Lodestone Perfume.

THE ANGEL

The herb Angelica is also known as Archangel and Masterwort. Among its many uses is exorcism, healing, visions, protection and luck. The root was used as a talisman among the Native American tribes. It was said when this root is carried in your pocket in a green bag it attracts gambling luck.

GAMBLING HAND

This well-known Voodoo spell works very effectively. Drill a hole in a nutmeg. Then fill this with quicksilver (also named mercury). Seal the hole with wax. Place into a mojo bag (one made of leather or the bag being the color green):

Lucky Hand Root
2 green or natural Lodestones
Silver Magnet Sand
Orris Root
Gold Magnet Sand
High John the Conqueror Root
Some Five Finger Grass
Devil Shoestring Root

Place the nutmeg into the mojo bag. Sew this closed. Next, sprinkle the mojo bag with Luck Oil at least once a week (on each Thursday and any other time you wish). Let no other person touch it. Carry this mojo bag at all times when you gamble.

MONEY POWDER

The money powder known as Algiers Powder also has varied other purposes. To use it for gambling luck, apply the powder to your hands before you try your luck at gambling.

If you are gambling in your home (card games, etc.), make a floor wash. Mix the Algiers Powder or Algiers Floor Wash with water. Then wash the floor in the room you will gamble with this. Next, sprinkle some of the Algiers Powder around the premises. This will remove bad luck.

FORTUNE DRAWING

Anoint the following items with the following oils all in the order in which they are stated.

Items: A $1 dollar bill, a silver quarter and a Buckeye.
Oils: Bayberry, Holy and Money Drawing.

Wrap the items in this manner:

Place the silver quarter with the eagle right side up and face down on left side of the dollar (so that it is aligned with the eagle on reverse of the dollar). Then place anointed Buckeye on top of the coin and roll the dollar bill from the left to the right so that the All Seeing Eye - Great Seal is showing and fold the ends to make it compact. Tape to ensure it is secure.

Place this in a green mojo bag which has Chamomile, Sage and Marigold herbs in the bottom of the bag and some other money. Anoint the contents as well as the inside seems of the bag with Power oil. Carry this with you at all times.

MONEY FROM DICE

If you gamble with dice, first wash your hands in tea made from Jezebel Root. Carry a John the Conqueror Root in your pocket next to your wallet. When you throw the dice, place your thumb on the root and call the number right before throwing.

GAMBLING FLOW

Sprinkle 7-11 Gambling Powder on your hands and charm bags before gambling. Focus on which method you want to win with (cards, dice, etc.).

DRAGON'S MAGNET

1. Take the stone Turquoise, wrap it in a small piece of material the color of gold. Anoint these with Success Oil.

2. On white paper, with black ink draw what area you need gambling luck in, such as, draw a pair of dice, a card, a lottery ticket. Next to this on the same piece of paper draw a horseshoe shaped magnet and a money symbol (such as a dollar sign $).

3. Place this on top of the material covered Turquoise. Next take another piece of gold material and wrap this around this mixture of items.Again anoint with Success Oil and focus on a large dragon bringing you all the money and luck you need.

4. Carry this with you when you gamble. Visualize the dragon being with you the whole time you gamble and say:

As sure as the sun rises in the east,
My dragon (make up a name for your personal dragon),
Brings me luck and fortune,
And power to overcome negativity,
As I say, So It Is.

TEA OF LUCKY CHANCES

Make a tea from the herb called Indian Root. When done, take the herb and carry it. Use the Indian Root as a floor wash if you are playing games of chance in your home. The herb can also be carried in a green pouch.

FIRE AND FLAME

To call down the thunder of Thor, use this ritual. Light a white candle and a green candle. Burn these on a Thursday. Focus on the candle flames. Visualize a jagged bolt of lightning coming down from above and into both candle flames. Visualize luck for gambling coming through the bolts of lightning and into the candles. Say:

Through the Fire,
And through the Flame,
Gambling luck comes to me from Thor,
And as it passes from lightning to flame,
I acquire all of Thor's luck and more.

Put the candle flame out after 15 minutes. Do not blow on it. Your breath will cancel the spell. Wait for the candle drippings to dry a little and take some of each candle. Put them into a white piece of material and carry it.

One of my clients used my Fire and Flame ritual when he went to Atlantic City. He went normally every other month. He very rarely won yet he loved going and wished he could at least do well one time. He used this ritual and for the first time he not only won, but won so much money that it was more than he could imagine.

This is a ritual of force so you would not utilize it all the time. He put some of the money he won back into aiding others and so kept the flow going. To this day he gambles with my ritual at times but he no longer has the need to gamble for getting *"a little past survival"*. He finally hit it big.

GAMBLING MOJO BAG

In a green conjure bag, carry the stone Turquoise and a green Lodestone. Carry this when you gamble. It will increase the percentage of times you win.

GLYPH OF LUCK

One of the strongest talismans for gambling is one that you make up yourself. Take the initials of your name and write them next to each other on white paper with green ink. Over these initials, write the number 7. Sprinkle with Lucky Hand Powder. Place this in your wallet and carry.

MAGICK VERSE

There is power in the word. This we are aware of. Magick verse is musical or rhythmic poetry. The verse uses similes, symbols and analogies. The verse is meant to get rid of a hex or cure ailments, do weather work, to gain control over a person or a situation, do positive spiritual work and elevation and to bring luck. Although magickal verses are associated more with pagan work, it is not limited in this manner. Originally the Psalms in the Bible were used with a musical background. Even now, these are known to heal sickness. Due to the "power of the word", you can make up your own and specify that it brings in gambling luck and ability and at the right time to you. Make sure it rhymes and says simply what it is you want. Be rhythmic. Be exact. The power and force of suggestion and manifesting is there.

JAMAICA GINGER SPELL

Take some Jamaica Ginger and a picture of a black cat and one of a bat. Place these in a red charm bag. Sew the bag closed with white thread. Anoint the bag every seven days with seven drops of Winners Circle Oil. Carry this for winning at games of chance.

MAGNETIC HORSESHOE

On a piece of orange paper draw a picture of a horseshoe with green ink. Above the horseshoe, still in green ink, write the number 7. Below it write the number 9. On the left of it write a money symbol such as a dollar sign ($). On the right of it write an arrow pointing up. Anoint this paper with Gamblers Oil every seven days. Focus on what you want. And carry it in your pocket or pocketbook.

LOTTERY WIN

Take Lucky Hand Powder and sprinkle it on your lottery ticket. Next, take Lucky John the Conqueror Oil and rub the oil along the edges of the ticket. Start at the left top corner and rub towards the right until you are at the same corner where you started. Do not lift your finger away from the ticket until you are done. You cannot break the line of energy flow. While you do this, focus on luck and abundance coming to you. See yourself happy. Plan what you will do with the money when it comes in for you.

LUCK OF THE SAINT

In a white handkerchief, in the center, place the image of St. Joseph, some Alfalfa, an Ankh and a parchment paper with your intent on it. Fold the handkerchief so that all of the items are covered. Place it under your mattress for nine days. Thereafter, every time you play a game of chance, carry it with you.

DICE LUCK

Place a pair of dice and two Tonka Beans and the Seal of Jupiter in an orange conjure bag and carry it when you gamble. Start to carry it two days before.

PERSONAL GAMBLERS CHARM BAG

In a green mojo bag, place the following:

2 Lodestones
pinch of Cinnamon
Apple Blossom
Rosemary
Pine

Next, place a small set of dice into the bag. Take a quarter and add it in. Add Anise on top of this in the mojo bag. Find something of yours that has brought you luck. If it is a shirt, as an example, cut a small piece from it and place it in. If it is something large or an object you cannot do this with, then take a photograph of it and place the photo into the mojo bag. Tie white string around the bag to seal it with eight knots. Carry this at times of gambling.

GAMBLER'S WISHES

For magickal use with gambling wishes, take the plant known as the Dandelion (also known as Priest's Crown and Wild Endive) and bury it at the northwest corner of your house. Make your gambling wish. Next, take some more of the plant and dry it out. The dried Dandelion is to be placed in your wallet. Make the same gambling wish you make when you buried the other Dandelion. This will ensure that the money you win will stay with you long enough to get home (rather than gambling it away again first). You can also place the Dandelion you carry in a small red bag sewn together with white thread. Do only one wish at a time.

HERBAL SPELL - GAMBLING

Take Irish Moss and carry it after you have said to it:

As the earth,
Is filled with gold,
So grows my wealth,
For all to behold.

From sun to sun,
From dusk to dusk,
May this spell,
Bring gambler's luck.

INFLUENCE IN GAMBLING

In a green mojo bag place a green rabbit's foot, 2 lodestones and the Seal of Fortune. Tie the mojo bag and anoint it with Fast Luck Oil. Then when you are ready to gamble, use a little of the Fast Luck Oil on the palms of your hands and wrists. Remember to focus your intent.

TO ATTRACT MONEY AND LUCK

On parchment paper, write the amount of money you need. Use Dove's Blood Ink. Focus your intent. Write a realistic amount for a purpose, such as to cover a bill. Be specific. If you write "I want to be rich", it can mean different things, varied levels, and it will be too scattered. Place the parchment near Money Drawing incense and burn it for nine days. After nine days you can use this parchment as a seal of Good Luck. Carry it eith you near your money when you gamble or add it to the contents of a lucky mojo bag.

LUCKY HAND OF CHANCES

Place the following items in an orange conjure bag:

1 Four Leaf Clover (real, drawn or object)
pair of Lodestones
Burning Bush herb
Grains of Paradise
Mustard Seed
Lucky Hand

Hold the conjure bag in your hand; focus your intent into it. Anoint it with Success Oil. Carry it at all times.

CHAPTER 8

MASTERING PROSPERITY IN BUSINESS

Numerous business people use varied forms to manifest in their financial lives. Businessmen use it to influence negotiations, to move up in their positions or to start new endeavors. Part of good business is to know when to make moves and when to escalate your creative ideas. A practitioner is very serious about the work that is being done. The metaphysician is always dealing from a positive, definite attitude, always from a quiet and serious outlook. Of course, we only deal from the positive side, the side of Divine Power.

You can manifest for yourself or others, but only from the outlook of a Light Worker. The metaphysician has complete trust in the reality of the Spiritual planes, the Divine Power and knows that he/she can influence these planes. When manifesting, remember the saying that when one door closes, another door opens. You can attract the right situations to you.

ENERGY STREAMS
MOTHER NATURE'S PARTY LINES

The energy currents have been utilized for centuries by Magi, High Priests, Priestesses and others of higher awareness levels. These energy streams, rivers and waves are an invisible force that flows over and under the earth's surface. Think of them as a network of crossing lines of energy spaced at varied intervals. They are fixed and thus over the centuries will remain in the same place. When these streams of mother earth are felt or seen psychically, they would appear much as a grid fixed in space. The energy streams are a natural part of the environment.

Much as they are always there, unseen physically, we are able to find them. There are several methods, one such method being a dowsing rod specifically programmed for this purpose by a dowser. Another way is to have a psychic or someone sensitive to these energies look for them. These currents have more of an influence in our lives than people realize. They are positive energy lines and have several effects known to us as occultists. Their vibrations affect plant life, animals, sea life and us. They can cause mood, attitude, mental and health changes, depending on where you are located. As an example, a person living in a house located within an energy stream would have a more positive attitude, be healthier and have more of a happy, joyous character. While this same person never living in the currents would be more depressed, could be a criminal or have ill health or what some term as bad luck.

In these days of more mobility and easier travel, we are not as stationary and the effects may not be as noticed or as influential. However, if you are aware, as an example, that you are not in an energy stream in the place you rented for your business and it is not working well at all, you can change locations thus improving your business. Have you ever noticed how there may be one store that has a constant change of owners over a short span of years, each owner selling various products that did not work out? Yet the location could be on a busy street. Logically, not all the products could be non-profitable. Yet when these same people relocate, their business improves.

There are many aspects of nature used by the Magi and High Priestesses consciously. The more aware you are about the environment and what is going on around you, the more you can work with the Law of Nature to improve your life. Work on always being positive, improving your life and staying on the Path of Light. The energy streams can be used consciously. If you are looking for a new business location, check the neighborhood to see how many previous owners were on that location and in what amount of time. Look at the person's mood who owns the spot now. Is it positive but edgy? Stressful? How do you feel when you go into the building? The Rooms? Use the knowledge consciously to give yourself and edge in business.

NOT TO BE DOMINATED

In making money, one of the important qualities you need to have is the ability not to let others (a boss, etc.) dominate or control you. If you allow them to, they will limit your movement up in a company, your level of income, use your ideas and say it is theirs (so they will move up on your creative concepts) and in general you will have a difficult time. You will be restricted.

To counteract this and to attract good fortune, consecrate the stone called Jasper. This stone is especially good for people in the sign of Sagittarius and Virgo.

DECISIONS

To make quick, alert business decisions, consecrate the stone called Aquamarine.

BUSINESS EXPANSION

Place the following herbs in a dark green bag and keep it in your desk at your place of business.

Golden Seal, Pecan, Wheat,
Black Snakeroot, Rice, Mint, Dill

Anoint the bag once a week with Money Drawing Oil. Place it somewhere that others will not see it.

GAINING A JOB

Put all your focus into the spell. When it is done correctly, there aren't any obstacles in your way.

1. Burn one knob of a green 7-knob candle for seven nights consecutively, after you anoint the candle with Success Oil.

2. Burn Fast Luck incense.

3. Bathe in Money Drawing Bath Salts. You only need one tablespoon in your bath water. Do not take a bath at this time. Only soak, with water up to your neck, for 15-20 minutes. Concentrate on your intent.

4. Think positive. Now go out and look for your right job.

SPELL TO INCREASE BUSINESS

Before you open your place of business to clients, sprinkle some Jinx Removing Salts at your front door. Then sweep it away. Next, sprinkle Silver Magnetic Sand from the front door to your cash register. Now, put a Buckeye and an Orris Root in the back of your cash register. Leave it there at all times.

PERSONAL MONEY MAGNET

1. Copy the picture of the magnet.
2. Sprinkle it with Money Drawing Powder.
3. Add your name to the picture.
4. This will draw prosperity and good fortune to you. Carry this in your wallet or purse at all times. Make a second copy and after fixing it, leave it at your place of business.

TO CONJURE MORE OR BETTER BUSINESS

1. Anoint a green conjure bag with Money Drawing Oil.
2. Place inside the bag two Lodestones, Patchouli and Lavender herb.
3. Hide the conjure bag in a dark place for seven days. Then carry it with you every day.

LUCKY BUSINESS

In a green mojo bag, combine the following:

Alfalfa
2 Lodestones
1 small magnet
Seal of Fortune
Buckeye - wrap a one dollar bill around it

Anoint the bag with Fast Luck Oil. Carry it with you.

MONEY ATTRACTION

At your place of work, place a green or white conjure bag where it will not be seen. Place the following items in the bag:

1 green rabbit's foot
1 orange rabbit's foot
2 Lodestones
1 Bloodstone
1 Moonstone
1 five dollar bill
A pinch of Fenugreek

Anoint the bag with Success Oil each day.

TO MAKE GOOD BUSINESS JUDGMENTS

Take a piece of parchment paper. Upon this write your name seven times. Over your name, draw a picture of an eel. Fold the parchment and carry it in your wallet or in your pocketbook.

RITUAL BATH FOR SUCCESS IN WORK

When you are seeking a new job, working towards a promotion or a raise, this is what is needed.

> Make chamomile tea by boiling one cup of water and two tablespoons of the chamomile flowers. Boil for 15-20 minutes with a lid on the pot. (Do not boil in aluminum pots.)
>
> Pour the strained liquid into your bath water. Use enough water to immerse yourself up to your chin. Soak for 20 minutes, focusing on your intent. When you are finished, do not towel dry yourself; let yourself air dry.

You will be surprised at how fast this works when you use it with confidence.

ATTAIN BUSINESS AMBITIONS

1. Do this Spiritual Work on a Sunday. In a box or pouch, place a one dollar bill that has been blessed.
2. Add a bird's feather and a Seal of the Sun.
3. Add a Clear Quartz Crystal and a Turquoise stone.
4. Add Golden Bough herb on top.
5. Seal everything (box edge, top of pouch) with green candle wax that has been melted over it.
6. Tie a white cord around it with seven knots.
7. Focus your intent with prayer.
8. Bury the box next to your place of business. Do not tell anyone.

QUICK BUSINESS DECISIONS

Consciously pre-program your subconscious mind. Focus on when you want a "yes" answer to a question, your right hand will warm up. When your answer is "no", your left hand will warm up. Another way you can program your hands is *hot* = *yes* and *cold* = *no*. You are linking into your Higher Self and Divine Power for the answer.

If you need to know if your promotion is coming in soon, ask it as a question. Then pay attention to the response yoou've programmed. Do this a few times for practice. Once you get the correct answers frequently, then you are tuned into your Source.

ATTRACT MONEY AND BUSINESS

This ritual must be done on a Thursday. To attract money and business, do the following:

1. Cover your altar woth a purple cloth. Light Cinnamon incense.
2. Place an Amethyst cluster on your altar.
3. Blend together in a bowl Cedar chips, Saffron spice and Star Anise.
4. Light a purple candle and invoke your desires.

Repeat this ritual every Thursday until you are satisfied with the results. When your altar is not active, either leave your ritual objects on it or put them away so nobody sees or touches them. Do not use the objects for any other purpose between Thursdays.

BUSINESS DRAWING

Place Lovage around your cash register or behind it. Place High John Root and Southern John Root inside the cash register.

VISUALIZE YOUR WAY TO WEALTH

Visualize yourself surrounded by orange, green and pink light each time you are at work. Visualize yourself in just the orange and in white light the rest of the time. Focus on money building so that it overflows in your wallet, home and bank. Ask it to come to you through Divine Power and Nasi each morning and each night.

MONEY OF THE KABBALAH

To attract riches, happiness and satisfaction. Use a grass green or deep green altar cloth.

With white chalk, write the letter "G" in the right upper corner and the number "7" in the left upper corner.

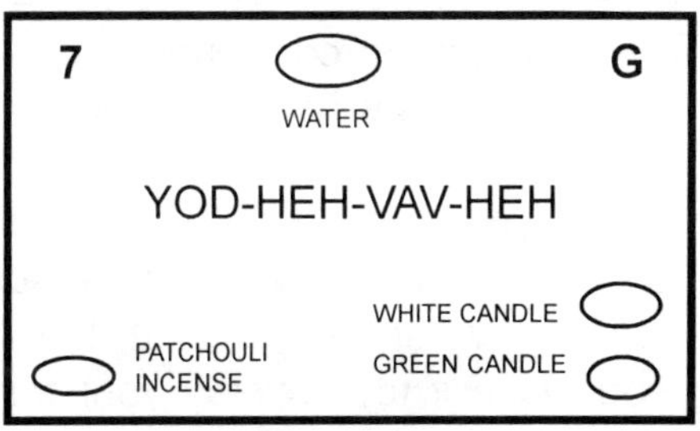

In the center, write "YOD-HEH-VAV-HEH".

Place a white and a green candle in the right bottom corner. Anoint with Success Oil.

In the left bottom corner place Patchouli Incense. Place a glass of water at the center top. At the center bottom, a feather. (Represents the elements)

Allow your body to feel an increasing chill. Focus on Divine Grace, on Will, Intellect, Your Feelings, Consciousness of As Above So Below. Then focus on your intent. Take your time.

THE LAW OF ABUNDANCE

This is also known by the name of the Law of Ten Fold. Any paper money that goes out will be affected. This also works with checks and money orders and credit cards (fold your receipt).

First, hold the bill in front of you. Use one dollar so you can see what I mean. Hold it so you can read the word "one dollar". This way it will come back to you. Faced in the other direction, you will notice it looks as though it is leaving. Now say to yourself:

Bless this money,
And as it goes out,
It comes back ten fold.

What it actually means in the first part is that you acknowledge where it comes from - God. The second line means you're manifesting it to come back now, not 20 years from now. The last part is "how" it will come back.

As you give someone the dollar, visualize ten dollars coming back to you at the same time, such as a ten dollar bill with wings coming over it towards you. It is said that this method will always work. Use it to increase your finance in business. Do this every single time you pay for anything.

SPIRITUAL ATTRACTION

Within 24 hours of a new moon, use or draw a check. Where it says "amount" write the amount you need and *"PAID IN FULL".* Make the check out to yourself (fill in name). Put the word *"TODAY"* where the date is written. As for the signature of who made out the check, write *"BANK OF UNIVERSAL ABUNDANCE".* When you are done, put it in your Bible.

MOVING THE OPPOSITION

If you want a promotion and you have competition you may not be able to overcome, do the following with seriousness, positive intent and through the use of White Light, Divine Power and In A Perfect Way.

First, say a prayer to request your desire.

Next, write the person's name on a piece of paper and focus the following intent onto it (and on the person if you see him/her):

Visualize the situation as it would come up (such as both of you being called to an office to be told about the decision). Visualize yourself being very happy with getting it. Shake the person's hand and thank him/her for giving you the position. Look at your opposition and become aware of how happy this person is, because he/she has another opportunity he/she would rather take. Shake the person's hand also and be a good winner. Walk out of the office and think of all you will do now. Feel elated! Successful! Get excited!

Rerun this scene to see it, feel it, know it. You can also visualize another, better opportunity for your opposition elsewhere prior to a decision being made. Visualize this person taking it happily.

Incorporate this method with a formula if you would like to. As long as you move your opposition in a positive way, to their Higher Good, you will do very well.

CHAPTER 9

NUMEROLOGY & MONETARY STRATEGIES

Numerology is the study of numbers. It is a science and utilized in occult. The numbers tell the person's character and life plan (destiny). Each number has its own characteristic and its own separate meaning. Each number contains a separate cosmic vibration and rhythm. Practical use of these specific functions have been with us from time immemorial. The vibrations of these numbers are connected on multi-levels. The numbers are ruled by planets and when you add these qualities to the number, you understand them better. Numbers are also connected to colors, plants, Tarot, Runes, deities, to name a few. Some people have lucky numbers. The numbers on the house you live in have influences on you. The house number can actually make you luckier. Reading correspondences is an art. Numbers connect to the Law of Magnetic Attraction. Written numbers go back to Egypt, Sumeria, China, among other places. To utilize numbers with force will gain the ability for you to plan better, avoid negative situations and improve your life.

HOW TO FIND YOUR BIRTHDATE NUMBER

The birthdate needs to come down to one number (from 1 to 9). To find your birthdate, use this method:

Add:	Your birth month
+	Your birth date
+	Your birth year
	Reduce the total to one digit.

As an example, if your birthdate is 3-15-1978:

Add:	3
+	15
+	1978

1996 = 1 + 9 + 9 + 6 = 25 which brought down to a single digit would now be 2 + 5 = 7.

Thus, your destiny number would be **7**.

GAMBLING

Any number in your birthdate is "lucky" for you, such as in the previous birthdate; 3, 1, 5, 15, 9, 7, 8 or any combination such as 113, 17, etc. Also, you will find these numbers will show up in your life more frequently in varied situations.

IVORY OF WEALTH

Carry a piece of Ivory and wrap it in a cloth the color of royal purple. Best days are: 9th, 18th, 27th.

AMULET FOR GAMBLING GAIN

Before gambling:

1. Take a bath in Red Clover and Fast Luck bath salts.
2. Wash your hands in a strong tea of Chamomile.
3. Make a mojo bag of the following ingredients:

Dragon's Blood Reed wrapped in a dollar

A Black Stone for protection from loss

A Buckeye for luck.

A Seal of the Sun with your name and birthdate on the back

6	32	3	34	35	1
7	11	27	28	8	30
19	14	16	15	23	24
18	20	22	21	17	13
25	29	10	9	26	12
35	5	33	4	2	31

Seal of Sun

4. To consecrate the seal place it under Yellow candle anointed with Sun Oil and burn Sun Incense.

NUMBERS OF THE ANGELS

Numbers are also influenced by different planes. Since we know that numbers connect to angels, we also know the purpose of the numbers by being aware of the sector and ability of the angels.

ANGEL	NUMBERS	INFLUENCES
Cassiel	15, 21	*Property, house, land, farm*
Sachiel	14, 18	*Expansion, money, powerful business associates, legalities, financial crisis, gambling*
Michael	11, 19	*Positions of Power*
Gabriel	2, 7,12,18	*Increase*

Use this knowledge when working with timing, rituals, formulae etc.

ATTRACT GOOD FORTUNE INTO YOUR HOME

Take a square of Parchment and write the following numbers in Dove's Blood Ink. Begin with number 1 and end with 16. As you draw your number square chant:

4	9	2	14
3	5	16	10
7	12	13	6
11	1	8	15

Athena, Goddess of light and home,
bless this house and all who live in it!

Now turn the Parchment over and draw an outline of your house, it 3 circles drawn clockwise and beginning with the outermost circle.

Repeat the invocation and burn Money House Blessing Incense while you do so.

IMPROVING WITHOUT MONEY

In the time of the Incas, early Native Americans, Egyptians and now in today's times, the barter system has more influence than people realize. In earlier times when money was not used they exchanged abilities or products such as eggs, wheat or shoeing a horse. Often you have an ability or commodity that you can utilize that somebody else may need. That, in fact, is money exchange.

Look at yourself and take inventory. What do you have as an ability or product? What about your needs? Who could supply them? How do they work and what could you do in return?

If you can do taxes, maybe you can get somebody who cuts hair from their home to exchange. You can do the person's taxes. This person can do a certain amount of haircuts for you to balance it out. The barter system is still in use. Take advantage of it. Make it work for you.

SOME POWDERS TO DRAW MONEY

The powders mentioned below can be found in any well-stocked occult supply store. Sprinkle throughout your home and place of business

Prosperity	*Good Luck*	*Zodiac*	*Command*
Money Drawing	*Come To Me*	*Van Van*	*Wealthy Way*
Success	*Magnet*	*Power*	*Lodestone*
Attraction	*High John*	*Fast Luck*	*Lucky 9*

Blend them in groups of 3, 9, 12. Mix the powders thoroughly together. Sprinkle them about your location. Visualize receiving lots of money.

TIGER ENERGY

Carry a picture of a tiger (in color). On the picture, sprinkle some Magnet Powder and Success Powder. Also some Good Luck Powder.

On a piece of white paper, draw the symbol of the sun (a circle with a dot in the center), your religious symbol (like a cross), and something to represent money (like a dollar sign $).

Wrap the white paper around the tiger picture and carry it in your wallet. This is to bring in luck, success and money.

EARTHLY GOODS

To heighten property and financial blessings, on a Friday, focus your intent and a symbol (square for earth) onto a piece of copper. Best days to use this: 6th, 15th, 24th.

YOUR FORTUNATE NUMBERS

These methods based on the Science of NUMEROLOGY are different for every person. The author has spent many years studying the occult meaning of numbers, and while we do not guarantee results, many use them with great success.

WHAT YOU MUST KNOW

First: Learn how to tell magic time. Numbers inside circle represent A. M. - just like a watch. Numbers outside circle represent the time after noon. ALWAYS NOTE HOUR.

MAGIC TIME

A. M. - 1-2-3-4-5-6-7-8-9-10-11-12

P. M. - 13-14-15-16-17-18-19-20-21-22-23-24

Second: Note the day of the week. Monday is 1; Tuesday is 2; Wednesday is 3; Thursday is 4; Friday is 5; Saturday -is 6; Sunday is 7.

Third: Count the number of letters in your name. *Example*: Jack Brown has four letters in his first name and five in his second name. 4 plus 5 equals 9. This number 9 is always lucky for Jack Brown.

Fourth: A lucky number is found by combining the values of .the day and month in which you were born. *Example:* If you were born on June 25th (June is the 6th month). combine 6 and 25 - thus 625 or 67. Add these figures: 6 plus 2 plus 5 equals 13. Add again, 1 plus 3 equals 4. This gives four magic numbers, all with the same strength: 625, 67, 13, 4. Use the one that suits you best. January equals 1; February 2; March 3; April 4; May 5; June 6; July 7; August 8; September 9; October 10; November 11 (or 2); December 12 (or 3).

FOUR METHODS FOR USING YOUR FORTUNATE NUMBERS

1. The Magic Hour: Use the number of the day of the week and the number of the hour at which you play or bet. Example: Suppose it is 4 P. M. on Friday (see clock.) 4 P. M. is 16 o'clock; Friday is 5. Combine these to make 165 or 75. Then add 1 plus 6 plus 5 equals 12. Add again, 1 plus 2 equals 3. This gives four magic numbers: 166, 75, 12, 3, with the same strength. Use the one that suits you best.

2. Strike The Keynote: Use the number of letters in your name and the hour of play. Suppose Jack Brown (9) wants a Lucky Number at 8 P. M. Combine 9 and 20 to make 920. Add these: 9 plus 2 plus 0 equals 11. Add again, 1 plus 1 equals 2. This gives four magic numbers: 920, 29, 11, 2. Use the one that suits you best.

3. Your Pinnacle of Success: Use the number of the day on which you were born and the number of the month. Suppose you were born on August 24th. Combine 24 and 8. This gives 248 or 68. Add 2 plus 4 plus 8 equals 14. Add again, 1 plus 4 equals 5. This gives you four Lucky Numbers of the same magic power: 9,48, 68, 14, 5.

4. Lady Luck Method: Count the number of letters in your sweetheart's name and combine with the number of letters in your own name. Example: Maybelle Jones (13 letters) and Jack Brown (9 letters) makes 139 or 49. Add these: 1 plus 3 plus 9 equals 13. Add again, i plus 3 equals 4. This gives you four Lady Luck numbers: 139, 49, 13, 4. Use the one that suits the occasion best.

NOTE: If you want more than one Lucky Number in a day, combine your Lady Luck number with the hour. Example: At 20 o'clock (8 P. M.), combine Maybelle Jones (13) with Jack Brown (9) : 20, 139. Add these to suit your convenience. ALWAYS NOTE THE HOUR. The time figure changes only when the hour changes. Adding, transposing or combining a magic numbdr does not alter its strength. Example: 165, 75, 12, or 3. Also a zero in a number can be used or not-204, 20, 2

LUCKY AND UNLUCKY DAYS

To ascertain the lucky days of any month, consult the almanac and find the date of the full moon. Then multiply the number of days in the month by the number of days occurring after the full moon. The digit should, if possible, be coupled, and if this is not possible, the first or second two should be transposed. Otherwise, each will indicate the lucky days. Thus, if the product is 418, the lucky days are the fourth and the eighteenth. If the product is 481, the lucky days are the same, as the 8 and 1 should be transposed. Should the result be 388, the lucky days would be the third and eighth, the latter being doubly lucky.

These, however, if they coincide with the unlucky days, determined by multiplying the number of days in the month by the number occurring before the full moon, must be disregarded and stricken out.

CONCLUSION

The person whose hands this book comes into is warned to use the Higher information and formulae for ONLY positive uses. Karma is a very intense force. In Karmic belief, every man and woman is responsible for their own actions. What you do will always come back. As in science: cause and effect.

So stay on the Path of Light. Success depends greatly on your connection with the Higher Force. Know in your heart that you truly deserve the best. Balance yourself and move on your feelings and wisdom. A magi is able to quickly size a situation up and immediately spring into action. If there is a problem or things are not progressing the way you want, take care of it. Change it!

Thrive on knowing you are a creator of your directions in life. You are the only one who has mastery over your life. Now is the time to create a new future of inner and outer wealth. Go forth as a Light Worker. The Universe yields to you!

ABOUT THE AUTHOR

Rev. Maria Solomon, better known by her former surname, "D'Andrea", was born in Budapest, Hungary. Since early childhood, she has demonstrated a high degree of psychic ability. As an Ordained Minister and Pastoral Counselor, Maria has provided excellent psychic guidance and enlightenment to many.

Rev. Maria's psychic abilities and talents over the past twenty-five years include: Crystal Gazing, Rune Casting, Biorhythm, Handwriting Analysis, Numerology, Trance States, Automatic Writing, Occultism, Tarot Card Reading, Kirlian Photography, the teaching of Psychic and Metaphysical techniques, Yoga and meditation principles and techniques. Also does Chinese Qi Gong (Er Mei Therapy). She is a Certified Hypnotherapist and holds a Doctor of Metaphysics degree (Ms.D.). She is also an Ambassador in Ministry, Principal Teacher in ISA and holds the titles of D.D. and D.R.H. She has been a guest speaker at metaphysical and occult organizations throughout the United States. She has also published articles on spiritual and pastoral guidance in numerous magazines and professional journals and continues to do so today. Among her credits are numerous appearances on radio and television shows.

Rev. Maria is the founder of the Sylvan Society - a hermetic order, a member of the Spiritual Frontier Fellowship, the Floating Healing Meditation Circle, the Life Study Fellowship, the Psychic Guild, A.R.E. (the Association for Research and Enlightenment), the Ghost Research Society and the Long Island School of Applied Hypnosis. She is an honorary member of the Tucscarora Indian Tribe.

Rev. Maria Solomon can be reached by writing to her at
2 Fanwood Place
S. Huntington, NY 11746